D0612882

The Germans and
Their Modern History

The Germans and
Their Modern History

Fritz Ernst

TRANSLATED FROM THE GERMAN BY

Charles M. Prugh

Columbia University Press
New York and London 1966

Dr. Fritz Ernst was professor of medieval and modern history at the Ruprecht–Karl–Universität from 1937 to 1963, and also served as Rector of the University from 1961 to 1963.

The original German title is *Die Deutschen und ihre jüngste Geschichte*.

Translator's Preface

The spacious New Auditorium of the Ruprecht–Karl–Universität (University of Heidelberg), which is well known to the generations of American students who, since 1931, have attended the University, was filled to overflowing as Professor Fritz Ernst ascended the rostrum in November 1961 to deliver the series of lectures translated and reproduced in this book.

Professor Ernst was born in Stuttgart in 1905 and studied in Tübingen, Berlin, and London. He taught in Buenos Aires in 1929–30 before becoming an instructor in history at the University of Tübingen in 1932. In 1937 he was called to the University of Heidelberg, where he held the chair of professor of medieval and modern history until his untimely death in December 1963.

During World War II his academic career was interrupted by a period of service in the German army, but he returned to Heidelberg and resumed teaching before the end of the war. He served two years as Rector of the University from 1961 to 1963; as administrative head he gained considerable distinction. The list of his many writings includes a number of books as well as contributions to various German historical journals. From 1938 on he also served as coeditor of the periodical, *Die Welt als Geschichte*.

Approximately a thousand students and several hundred

townspeople assembled each week during the winter semester to hear the Rector speak on "The History of the German People during the Past Fifty Years" ("Die Deutschen und ihre Geschichte in den letzten fünfzig Jahren").

If, as some have claimed, parents and teachers in the secondary schools of Germany have united in a "conspiracy of silence" on this subject, this silence was now to be broken. The noticeable eagerness of the students to listen was matched by the rapt attention of the representatives of the older generation. Although some had come out of mere curiosity, and others had come to find fault with the speaker's point of view, none could dispute the Rector's right to speak on the subject; none could question his reputation as historian and his competence to deal with the controversial issues that were to be discussed. He was tackling subjects he believed to be as important as life and death to the German people, for he too had lived through the catastrophes of the Third Reich; he too had survived the horrors and holocausts of World War II.

His ultimate target in these lectures was the minds and hearts of the students before him. As he explained to me on one occasion, he felt it to be his responsibility as Rector of this famous University to see to it that the students did not leave its halls without having heard a frank and factual report of what had actually happened and without having pondered their own personal responsibility in the emerging future of their Fatherland.

Immediately after its appearance at the Frankfurt Book Fair in the fall of 1963, the German edition of the lectures, called in book form *Die Deutschen und ihre jüngste Geschichte,* became a center of discussion and of controversy. For what the Rector had attempted was not merely a methodical narration of historical facts but rather a description of how these events affected the German people, their thinking, and their acting. "I must ask you to believe that I am trying to be as fair as possible. It is not my aim to split hairs, but to show that the

Germans as a people can and must come if not to a uniform at least to a prevailing interpretation of their history, if they wish to continue as a nation."

People all over the world who are concerned about democracy and about the threats to its survival will find this book of special interest. Here are answers to such persistent questions as: What effect did World War I have upon the Germans? Why did the Weimar Republic fail? Who was really responsible for Hitler? How was it possible for him to come to power? What effect did the Allied Occupation have upon the Germans after World War II? What about the future of the Federal Republic of Germany and its chances to become a bulwark of democracy in the heart of Europe?

It was one of Professor Ernst's last requests, made to me personally before his death just before Christmas 1963, that these lectures be made available to the English-speaking world. This request emphasizes the earnestness and passion that he put into the writing and delivery of these lectures, and it has been a source of considerable satisfaction to me to have been able to complete this task and to dedicate it to his memory.

CHARLES M. PRUGH

Heidelberg
August, 1965

Author's Preface to
the English Edition

This book consists of a series of lectures delivered in 1961–62 in the New Auditorium at the University of Heidelberg. Approximately 20 to 30 percent of the hearers were middle-aged and elderly people; the rest were students. The lectures were intended chiefly for the students and were meant to answer some of the questions young people have today.

It may be of some interest even to non-Germans to see what attempts are being made in Germany today to solve the problems of recent history. It will be clear to all that this is in no sense a "national apology." It is rather an apology of an older generation to a younger, an endeavor to make the young people understand what their parents and their older relatives lived through. Apart from the question of whether and to what extent this effort has been successful, it can certainly serve to testify to what is of concern to the Germans in their discussions at the present time. The phenomena of National Socialism, dictatorship, and of World War II are naturally the main points of interest, but these must be set into the larger context of the years since 1911.

Various occurrences in foreign lands within the past several decades have shown that other nations are also subject to trends which can endanger states founded upon the principle of justice and democracy. Only a little while ago the German people succumbed to such trends and under their domination became the aggressor against other nations. The tyrannical power that held sway in Germany was then imposed in other countries, and millions of people were persecuted and destroyed. It is understandable, therefore, that bitterness against the Germans, bitterness among the Germans, and bitterness among former Germans still exists today. Such antagonism cannot be explained away. But anyone, whether the persecuted and embittered, the outsider or the nonparticipant, who is interested in explaining at least some of these things (by no means all of them) may well find in what follows material for making his own analysis and interpretation.

FRITZ ERNST

October, 1963

Excerpts from Author's Preface
to the German Edition

To be sure, good manuals of the most recent history of Germany are available today, but so far as I know there is no adequate treatment of the manner in which the German people themselves experienced the happenings of the past half century.

There will of necessity be a certain degree of subjectivity implicit in any such presentation by a contemporary writer. Our concern here is not about which day Wilson announced his famous Points in their final, effective form, or when Hitler made his decision to invade Poland. What is of interest is the reaction of the German people, particularly of those classes of society that are comprehensible to us, to the events so far as they were publicly apparent and immediately operative.

Both the need for historical truth and the concern for the education of the youth of today demand that history be depicted as it was experienced. What was generally known among the people, and what could they find out? These are questions that must be asked if one would weigh, for example, what the theory of the "stab in the back" after 1918, or the concept "seizure of power" by Hitler meant to the experience of the German people. This should not lead to the complete exoneration of the people or, more specifically, of the middle class. But an effort should be made to impart something of the atmosphere that made the catastrophe possible —the victory of the theory of the "stab in the back," and the hopes centered on Hitler as the lesser of two evils in what seemed a hopeless situation.

A presentation such as this will of course suffer from the fact that many readers are not interested in the whole fifty-year span (1911–1961) that is comprehended here, but only in the problem of National Socialism. Yet the story of Hitler and of his successes cannot be understood without going back at least fifty years. A further elaboration of this I must deny myself. The historian can deal with the question of the "guilt" of the German people or of its middle class only when he has the material with which to make comparisons. What have other peoples felt in a similar situation; how did their responsible classes act? In a certain sense the French people seem to have had a history similar to ours, but I will only occasionally refer to the experience of other peoples.

It is also possible, and that is dangerous, to go too far to the opposite extreme of traditional patriotism by wallowing in the humiliation of the mistakes of one's own country and by applying to what has transpired standards that really cannot be applied. However, when we ask how these monstrous things could possibly have happened—when we seek to explain—

then we dare not shrink from passing judgment. Many Germans have forgotten today what they themselves said in 1946. Granted that many a statement made then was too severe, too one-sided; but to remain silent or to gloss over events as is presently being done, is just as one-sided and much more dangerous. Should such an attitude prevail, it would result in a horrible retribution.

Contents

The Germans and
Their Modern History

Introduction

Half a century ago! What prospects did the Germans have at the end of 1911?

It is easier to ascertain what the readers of German newspapers thought when they read about the disagreements over foreign policy than to determine what was actually shaping foreign policy. In November 1911, after lengthy resistance of the Germans, an agreement was reached with the French according to which the right to occupy Morocco and to establish a protectorate there was conceded to the French, and in return Germany was to receive a poor strip of land bordering on its existing colony of Cameroons.

That was the outcome of the second Morocco crisis, and the nature of the settlement was a symptom of the deteriorating state of the German Empire. Shortly before that, Italy, one of the two allies of Germany (Germany was a member of the Triple Alliance, along with Austria-Hungary and Italy), had staged a surprise attack upon the Turkish Empire in Tripoli, and in the Balkans aggression of a more serious nature was being prepared against the Turkish domination there. It was an unsettled time, to be sure, but the majority of the German people were not aware of the turmoil. Looking less at the tense international situation, they beheld only everyday Germany, German power, and the prestige and orderliness of the German monarchy.

Exactly forty years had passed since Bismarck had founded the Prussian-German Empire, and twenty-one years since Bismarck had been removed by the youthful German Kaiser, William II. Many sensed that in these twenty-one years German power had declined, but the feeling of order and safety was still widely prevalent. In November 1911 scarcely anyone in Germany could conceive the possibility that only seven years later, in November 1918, this German Empire would lie prostrate. There may have been individuals who foresaw doom; for example, a man named Oswald Spengler was sitting in his study in Germany concocting the basic ideas that he later amplified in his work, *Der Untergang des Abendlandes* [The Decline of the West], in which he endeavored to analyze not merely the state of Germany but of the entire Western culture. He later said that the lightning flashes of those months had given him the inspiration for it.

To bolster the sense of security, the summer of 1911 had been a warm and dry season; the wine had turned out unusually well, and like the winegrowers, who were exulting over their success, almost the whole of Germany felt content about the state of the economy. For in recent years Germany had become one of the leading industrial countries of the world. The centers of industry along the Ruhr and in Upper Silesia belonged to one of the largest economic conglomerations on earth.

The German Empire embraced 540,000 square kilometers. Its population was in excess of 65 millions and had increased at the rate of 1.5 percent annually in the last ten years. From 540,000 square kilometers—and here we must indulge in looking ahead—the size of Germany shrank to 470,000 square kilometers as a result of World War I. Today, the Federal Republic of Germany and the German Democratic Republic of Ulbricht together have about 370,000 square kilometers, of which the Federal Republic has not quite 250,000. Since 1911, then, political Germany has decreased from 540,000 square kilometers to 370,000 square kilometers, and an actually free German state is less than half the size of the German Empire of 1911. During World War II, a joke was being circulated. Goebbels said to Göring: "What are you going to do after the war?" "I shall ride through Germany on a bicycle," was the reply. "And what are you going to do that afternoon?" It did not actually turn out to be as bad as that, but it is bad enough.

Perhaps those who do not know this period through personal observation may have examined photographs taken during the years before 1914. The large German cities did boast modern department stores built in the style of the period, often in the most modern style, but apart from this the physi cal appearance of the cities was essentially the same as in 1880. The means of transportation had been partially modernized; electric streetcars could be seen side by side with horse-drawn carriages. The well off had for the most part gone over to the automobile. It was an automobile, however, which can be plainly seen to have been derived from the old horse-drawn wagon. The women wore broad hats and long dresses, the men wore tight-fitting trousers that had no crease in them, and the boys, at least those of the middle class, were clad in sailor suits. Class distinctions among adults were plainly to be observed in everyday life. Workmen could be easily distinguished from citizens of the middle class. They usually wore caps, whereas the middle-class citizens wore black, round, stiff hats in winter, and round, stiff straw hats in summer.

To return to the technical side. Long-distance travel was mostly by railroad, and the German long-distance express trains were quite efficient and were nearly as fast as they are today. Neither the automobile nor the truck was yet a match for the train. Although some airplanes were being flown for private sport, and some models of military planes were being tested, there was still no air transportation.

The German people and their history since 1911. . . . Why

did I choose a span of fifty years? For the simple reason that this time encompasses the decisive events without which our present-day world cannot be rightly understood. That I begin with the year 1911 means that I wish to include the last brief period before World War I. It does not mean that the year 1911 was necessarily an epochal year. But we need to go back this far because only thus can we grasp the effects of World War I on the German people. These experiences were the decisive factors that influenced the fate of the Weimar Republic as well as the domination of Hitler, in the shadow of which we are still living. I have therefore selected these five decades, because only in this manner can we understand the problem that confronts the Germans now.

But what actually is my purpose? Not a review of the events of the years since 1911 nor an attempt to analyze these events. Mine shall be a different kind of effort: to reveal along several major lines how the German people lived through these fifty years and how the nature of their experiences has influenced their history. I repeat, along several major lines, for I must confine myself to these from the very beginning.

What does "experience," a popular word of our time, really mean? It means: How did the people absorb these happenings? How did they interpret them, and how did they react to them? What kind of conclusions did they draw from them, and how did these regulate their future conduct? As will be noticed at once, we cannot be content merely with "experiencing," with living through something. For every experience in a situation of this sort leads to a certain type of behavior. To be more specific, the manner in which the majority of Germans reacted to the utter defeat of 1918 determined their attitude toward the Weimar Republic and toward Hitler. The way in which the majority of Germans reacted to Hitler determines their attitude down to the present day.

I should like to mention something that is still of basic importance: human beings undergo change as a result of what befalls them, of what they experience. Not as far as their essential makeup is concerned, but as far as what is visible or what they are conscious of is concerned. These changes shape future history, not these alone, but these also.

In September 1939 a Canadian wrote in a letter from France: "I ask myself how people will be when everything is over." "Everything" here means World War II, which had just broken out. How will people be? They would be different, at any rate.[1]

And an entire people? Can we speak simply, as we are doing, about a "German people"? What do we actually know about this people and about its so-called experience? What can we know about it? Well, so far as the most recent times are concerned, everyone knows something of what happened, at least in his own particular sphere. But what do we know about the people of 1914? Though people are still alive who lived through that time in full consciousness and who remember it, they have experienced other things in the meantime, and these new experiences have twisted their recollections of the preceding events. But we have more than mere memories of the older generation; we have many written records, letters and diaries that are genuine and unchanged.

This, however, leads to a certain restriction of the term "German people." These letters and diaries were written only by the so-called educated classes. Letters by people who were not accustomed to writing have been collected only in wartime and are usually of scant documentary value. On the other hand, written statements of the so-called educated people tell us something about the opinions of other social classes as well. Today we often speak of the democratization of the German people. But the unity of the German people in 1914 was an outgrowth of their basic presuppositions and of their common experiences, even more than is the case today. Thus, I shall rely mainly on the opinions of the German middle class as far as written sources are concerned. The middle class is the segment of society in which historical experience is reflected most clearly and by which it is assimilated in the most satisfactory manner. We shall see how the majority of the middle class misunderstood the decree that fate pronounced over them in 1918 and how this class, already inwardly endangered, paved the way for the accession of the power of Hitler, the most anti-middle-class power one can imagine.

How, then, will it be possible to treat in this short book such a huge subject, which is comparatively unexplored in its particulars and which is so controversial in general? I shall follow a procedure that will simplify matters and that has the advantage of bringing them more closely to your attention. Again and again I shall bring the expressions of individuals into focus and comment upon them. Although they are the statements of individuals, I shall try to make clear to you to what extent these expressions reflect the general opinion of the people or the opinion of one particular class. Only in this manner, with the help of citations, can we find a clue that will lead us through this vast field of inquiry. The selection of material to be quoted will depend on the period under discussion. For the twelve years of Hitler's regime they must be chosen with special care, and even then explanations will be necessary. There are comparatively few free, contemporary statements from the period of the dictatorship. What did the people think about it? The leading supporters of the regime expressed themselves for the most part with an eye to the effect of the moment; the opponents of the regime could not write open letters or genuine diaries because mail was censored and their homes might be searched. When they did make statements they often camouflaged them by ardently professing a belief in National Socialism. Only those who have experienced this entire period and kept a critical mind are in a position to pass judgment upon it.

Those who are seventy years old today were between twenty and twenty-five during World War I and for the most part had been soldiers in that war. But people who were older at that time still had recollections of 1870. Paul von Hindenburg was a lieutenant at the time of the proclamation of the German Empire in Versailles in 1871 and became a field marshal in World War I. He became president of the Weimar Republic and as such he appointed Adolf Hitler chancellor of the Reich. Those who are sixty-five years old today were soldiers at the end of World War I and some of these men fought in World War II. Those who are forty years old today grew up in the shadow of the aftermath of World War I and bore the major burdens of World War II. Those who are under thirty-five years old now went to school under Hitler; they may even have participated, at the end of the war, by becoming assistants to aircraft spotters. All who are younger than that have learned these things only from hearsay.

Finally, a personal word about myself as one who experienced this most recent history. In the days of the Weimar Republic I grew up to have something of a political sense. But I was educated in schools in which the dominant viewpoint was that of the so-called national middle class and I had convictions about the recent past that are today regarded by the vast majority of German historians as having had disastrous consequences. I assure you that it took a good deal of effort to rid myself of these convictions. Thus I do not belong to those who can speak with cold rationality and from a safe distance about, for example, the myth of the "stab in the back," [2] for I know what influence such national myths can have over a people. Perhaps the most difficult task I will have here is to make clear to today's youth that such sentiments as passionate love for one's country were an actual force, and that, even though they were badly directed, these feelings could be sincere and unselfish. It is even difficult for students today to grasp what the word "Fatherland" meant to earlier generations. But in discussing the structure and meaning of national emotions and how they were misdirected and misused, I do not wish to make you more skeptical than you already are. Skepticism sometimes flourishes in academic classrooms, but skepticism alone has never accomplished anything. Even in an age of international organizations love of one's country is in order, but it must be a love of one's country that is in harmony with a knowledge of history and of the world, and it must not throw overboard the simplest rules of reason. Ignorant passion and stupidity overcharged with feeling have never accomplished much and have nothing to do with genuine patriotism.

On the other hand, I must caution you against going too far to the other extreme. It did happen, in 1918—and at that time was opposed especially by Max Weber, as we shall see. In 1945 it became quite common for Germans to revel in the baseness of their fellow countrymen. This is understandable, when referring to the period beginning in 1933, but even so such an attitude is one-sided. Often the very same people who condemn their compatriots make exceptions of themselves and of their friends. In German literature there are significant voices that criticize the Germans. One could cite Goethe. But even there mistakes can creep in. The British prosecutor at the first Nürnberg trial quoted a passage from Goethe about the Germans that was devastating. But when someone bothered to look it up, it was found that it did not come from Goethe after all. The passage occurs in Thomas Mann's *Lotte in Weimar* [*The Beloved Returns*], in which Mann has Goethe speak. Even so the passage must be taken seriously, since it is by Thomas Mann, who always, even as an emigrant, had to contend with his attitude toward the Germans. But it just does not come from Goethe.

In casting aside his own people, a German who expresses such a negative viewpoint sometimes tells us more about his own torn soul than he tells us about the Germans themselves. All of which does not mitigate the fact that since 1933 things have happened in the name of Germany, and deeds have been committed by Germans, which even those in foreign lands who hated Germany most would not have believed possible. This condemnation is understandable, but it dare not be one-sided, and it must guard against easygoing Pharisaism.

In the following chapters I shall discuss the effect upon Germany of World War I and the effect of its outcome, I shall discuss the people during the Weimar Republic, the presuppositions regarding the rule of Hitler, the people under the dictatorship, and, finally, the year 1945 and the experiences the German people have had since that date. I shall choose the most significant pages, but I must make selections from them, and I assume, therefore, that particularly the older ones among my readers will not always agree with me when I discuss bygone days. I assure you that I shall compare my own political convictions, which I have already mentioned, with those of others, and I shall introduce as much material as possible from the literature that was at my disposal. No one today can possibly survey the entire body of literature from 1911 to 1961. In any case, personal observations will unavoidably appear from time to time, since every analysis of Germany's most recent history is nourished, intentionally or not, by personal impressions. I must ask you to believe that I am trying to be as fair as possible. It is not my aim to split hairs, but to show that the Germans as a people can and must come, if not to a uniform, at least to a prevailing interpretation of their history if they wish to continue as a nation. At times I shall mention other nations, but only by way of comparison, for our subject here is the German people.

Chapter One

The German People
on the Eve of World War I

When speaking about the German Empire today one must be aware of the existence of two distorted viewpoints. The one is positive and is found especially in older people who have conservative leanings and who are apt to glorify the past. In the old days, according to their way of thinking and talking, everything was better: the people were better, there was more law and order, there was still respect for authority, and Germany was powerful and great.

The last point cannot be denied, but around 1911 law and order were no longer so clear-cut and so secure as the people, particularly those who themselves profited from the stable order of things, would have us believe.[1] Germany was controlled by an aristocratic middle class; the civil service and the military were the leading professions. But things were beginning to change, and the system no longer suited the changing society. Many people were restless and dissatisfied, and among the governing classes this restlessness and discontent resulted in criticism of the Kaiser's personal methods, but they did not oppose the monarchy. The working classes, however, were against that form of government itself. The middle-class leftists were also against this form of government, but their criticism was more moderate. Generally speaking, the weaknesses of the government were yet to be revealed—by the war.

The other sort of distortion, which is more common today, is a negative one. In fact, the objections come from various sides and are about different aspects of the situation. For instance, regarding politics and sociopolitics, the opinion is that the Empire was unjust, a class state that had made the lower strata suffer. A similar criticism is that the Empire was an absolutism, governed by a small group close to the Kaiser. As to culture, it is said that the Empire lacked ideas, produced no art or good literature, was hollow and uncreative, and was essentially dominated by a hypocritical morality.

Just as the positive distortion has arisen from a one-sided idealization, so the negative distortion has arisen from many accurate but one-sided observations. These distorted observations have led to a judgment of the times that is too severe because it tends to accuse Germany alone. The same can also be said of remarks about culture and morality, for there were numerous and widespread intellectual movements before 1914 of which, later, people of the Weimar Republic were proud. The German Youth Movement, for instance, experienced its initial successes at that time. Hypocritical morality, as far as what has been said about it is valid, extended also beyond Germany's borders. Moreover, the Germany of 1914 was not a class state in a completely negative sense. It was rather a country whose government was based on a traditionally patriarchal order in which the social legislation founded in the Bismarck era was, at least in keeping with the thinking of the times, alleviating the condition of many poor people. But at the same time the lower classes were not represented adequately enough to be able to participate in the making of economic and political decisions, and it must be admitted that the individual citizen, even if he were a member of the upper classes, was less able to influence political decisions than his counterpart in France or in England. But here I must elaborate; one point must be made clear. Comparison with western Europe may have had significance for some politicians in the Empire, especially for the leftist liberals, who wanted a stronger parliament and pointed to the West in order to bring it about. But any comparison of his daily political life with western Europe had a certain unreality for the average German citizen before 1914. The vast majority, even those interested in politics, had eyes only on Germany—and this Germany was strong and great and properly administered; anyone, except the leftist liberals, who expressed criticism usually did so without comparing Germany with the West.

Those who were school children during World War I were convinced that everything German was absolutely and universally the best, from Krupp steel to German science, from the German army to Goethe and Schiller. It was not until 1918, when the western democracies and the parliamentary monarchies triumphed over Germany, that a large segment of society learned that comparison was possible. Before that, German national awareness, which was then only one generation old, had been so rigid—I shall not say strong and certain—had been so rigid that anything not German could be of no significance. The younger readers will hardly be able to grasp this, but we must see this difference clearly from the beginning, we must see how this change came about, or we shall not understand the essential.

Before 1914 two historical convictions had blended strangely and dangerously in the German consciousness. The one was the old, classical tradition that the Germans were more upright and more honest than foreigners—especially the French and the Italians—a view that had shortly before found expression in a saying by Geibel, "The world may one day find recovery in the German spirit." The other, a newer conviction from the period between 1871 and 1900, was that the German was the triumphant man, one who had founded his empire on victories and who, even in the economic sphere, had overtaken or at least caught up with the older powers.

The honest German belongs to the beginning of the nineteenth century: he has become the symbolic "Michel" who is outsmarted by others. The triumphant German of 1900, however, boasted that he was more successful than the others. The dangerous element here was that this newer self-image could be superseded at any time by the older one—whenever anything went wrong, the image of the honest and naive German manifested itself anew. But it must be said that many Germans even before 1914 were prouder of the good qualities attributed to the national character than they were of material success.

But comparison with the world outside was not really important. People had little concept of it. Though most Germans knew something about the French, and generally despised them, and a few had at least a vague conception of the English (English was hardly taught at all in humanistic secondary schools), only a handful had more than a superficial notion of the power of the Americans. When reports of political scandals in foreign lands appeared in all the newspapers, people said, "Such things do not happen here. We have law and order."

I cannot go into the constitutional foundations of the Empire; I can only touch upon several points. The German Empire was a constitutional monarchy in which the ruler was bound by a constitution (in contrast to the old absolutist monarchy as well as to the old forms of the class state). The passing of legislation and the adoption of the national budget were subject to the approval of the parliament, and the administration of the government was dependent upon the cooperation of ministers.

This government, although historic in form, allowed full play for possible action. The German Empire was a confederation; the Prussian king was at the same time the German Kaiser, and under him, though officially next to him, were the "confederate" princes of the other German states. It became increasingly clear, however, that the other states of the federation, with their courts, governments, and capital cities, were losing their importance. Thus the German Kaiser, particularly the last Kaiser, William II, became a figure of destiny.

It is still somewhat difficult today to speak calmly about William II in the presence of Germans who are more than fifty years old. During and after World War I he was so bitterly and so one-sidedly attacked by Germany's enemies as well as by the German leftists, that many people who up to the time of his downfall were counted among his critics came to his defense. People had at first greatly overestimated his actual power. One thing is certain: he did not want the war, and during it he suffered considerably. While he was an exile in Holland he had to witness the invasion of the Netherlands by Hitler's troops.

I remember a photograph in which he is striding along in front of an air force contingent exactly as he had before 1914—the *grand seigneur*—wearing white spats. On two occasions I saw him myself as a child. Actually only once, because the first time, when I thought the fancily dressed man atop the royal coach was the Kaiser, it proved to be only one of his courtiers in a hunting uniform, and unfortunately the maid gave me the information too late, and in the midst of the shouting I missed the real one. Perhaps she too was at first not quite certain and was herself charmed by the appearance of the bejeweled courtier.

William II is a figure not without tragic aspects, but certainly without greatness. Unhappy circumstances—a crippled left arm, the unfortunate relationship with his English mother, his Draconian upbringing—did not permit him to develop genuine self-confidence. He had dismissed Bismarck in the second year of his reign, a mistake which, however, was not entirely his own. He had reveled around 1900 in the successes achieved through the new naval and colonial policy, but by 1911 his initial enthusiasm had waned. At the time of the punitive campaign against the Boxers in China he urged the German troops in a memorable speech to fight like the ancient Huns so that the Chinese would come to have a lasting respect for the Germans. In other instances also he was too extravagant in his speeches, which were not well thought out and therefore immature.

Theobald von Bethmann-Hollweg, his chancellor in 1911, was a conscientious administrator of the Prussian noble type, but the Kaiser was influenced more by the attitude of the men of the court who had gathered around him. Among these were some who spoke to him in a cynical, ill-considered fashion about the world and about people; they thus encouraged him in his moods instead of pacifying him. This was a sharp comedown from the world of his grandfather, of Bismarck, and of the elder Moltke.

Something of the strength of the previous generation was still to be found in the former chief of staff, Alfred Graf von Schlieffen, who was alive and active though in retirement. Many loyal Germans watched this situation with mounting anxiety, but were unable to change it. For change was impossible under the Constitution, and so the Conservatives placed themselves behind the Kaiser with misgiving hearts. William II spoke and wrote English well, he had deep feelings for the country of his English mother, but it was a feeling of vindictive love. For the French he had only disrespect, and his attitude toward the Social Democrats of Germany was hostile, especially after early efforts to reach an understanding with them had failed. But of more importance is that he did not have the capacity to work hard; he was not stable and could easily be swayed. In his hands the monarchy would be endangered should a crisis develop—and a crisis did come in 1914. On the other hand, it would be difficult to maintain that a different ruler could have altered the course of things—there was too much confusion in the affairs of the state.

The atmosphere in the South German states was different. Of course it must be emphasized that the spirit of William II was no longer representative of the Prussia of former times, but was rather a combination of nearly parvenu boastfulness and of a somewhat frivolous officiousness. The kings of Bavaria and Württemberg, and the grand duke of Baden were loved by their people, and Social Democrats had access to their courts. The king of Württemberg could walk alone through the streets of his city unprotected by private detectives, and he acknowledged every greeting, though it made his walk somewhat strenuous. Here in the Southwest a liberal democratic spirit was noticeable, typical of the middle class and of the democratic traditions of these South German states. Here, and to a considerable degree in the Hanseatic towns of North Germany, more was known of foreign countries and of other peoples. But the foreign policy was shaped in Berlin, where the spirit, or lack of spirit, which surrounded the Kaiser reigned in spite of all the conscientiousness still to be found among German diplomats.

To the world, German foreign policy often appeared to be aggressive even when it was not meant to be, and this had its effect right up to the war. After the outbreak of the war two of the leading German diplomats, the ambassador in London, Prince Karl Max Lichnowsky, and the ambassador in Washington, Count Johann Heinrich Bernstorff, raised violent objections to the way in which German foreign policy had been conducted, stating that it only irritated Germany's allies without showing any real strength. Certainly no one in a responsible position in Germany really wanted war.

Nor did the people want war. To be sure, a strong and especially vocal group, known as the Pan-Germans, existed among the middle classes, who reveled in Germany's power and wanted to increase it. They wished for an inner revival of the nation, but, in their one-sided allegiance to the upper middle class and to the Officers' Corps, they never had the welfare of all the people in mind, and only contributed to the widening of the breach among the people instead of healing it. This group had no noticeable influence on policy, but leaders of foreign countries could point to their warlike utterances whenever they wished Germany to appear as a specter of terror. What must never be forgotten is that the founding of the Bismarckian Empire had created a new situation in Europe. With considerable foresight Bismarck had tried to consolidate Germany's new position of power. In the era of William II people considered it to be secure, and many, though not all, became careless.

But the real weakness of the Empire can be traced to the fact that though the people for the most part were politically mature, as far as their interest and their desire to take part in decision making was concerned, their influence on the government was slight. Parliament, that is, the Reichstag, could render the work of the government ineffective, but it could not form a government. Germany was not a parliamentary state but rather a constitutional state, and the majority of German citizens were actually proud of that fact and looked down on France and on England, and especially on the United States. Moreover, the populace felt that Germany was well administered—this was even true—but they failed to see that it was not well governed. For the most part, the bureaucrats and the Officers' Corps could not conceive of being dependent upon parliament to make ultimate decisions. Parliament was called the "gossip-chamber," and this was in keeping with the traditional German distrust of the spoken word.

Again a difference of attitude existed between the rest of the country, especially the southern sections, and Berlin. In South Germany the people were less intense, and placed less emphasis on power and on military form than in Berlin. Emphasis upon military matters was, to be sure, a Prussian tradition, but in the period of the Prussian reforms the effort had been made to combine militarism with national ideals. In the new Empire, however, too little was remembered of the era of Prussian reform, and often the elevation of the military went oddly hand in hand with the pride of the middle-class reserve officer, who, if possible, was also a member of an academic dueling fraternity.

I can give you only a brief outline here of the basic reaction of the German people to World War I. But even in such an abbreviated presentation it can be established that the German opposition, especially that of the Social Democrats, had, under the existing conditions, practically no prospect of ever participating in the government. Could the Kaiser be expected to appoint ministers who were Social Democrats? In the atmosphere of 1911 this appeared to be wholly impossible. This put the opposition of the Social Democrats in a peculiar situation and prevented them from gaining experience in government, even when they were strong enough, in 1912, to win the greatest number of seats in the Reichstag. They could, of course, give opinions on all the proposed legislation and even make weighty contributions to the discussion of the affairs of the army—but they were always in the position of a party that could never expect to take over the responsibilities of government. The same could be said of the left wing of the middle-class Democrats, whose situation was, however, somewhat different.

Generally speaking, it can be said that the vast majority of the people felt secure in the order of things, but this must be supplemented in order not to be misunderstood. In most countries of Europe, at least in the large ones, the same feelings prevailed, though less so in the countries of the Austro-Hungarian monarchy with which imperial Germany was allied. This must be explained further. The feeling of security must not be confused with the quiet of a cemetery. New life had made itself felt in the intellectual realm since the turn of the century, and something was brewing in the political sphere, even though opportunity to change the existing form of government was remote. But even those responsible for this ferment, especially the socialists, could scarcely believe in the possibility of changing the existing conditions in the foreseeable future. There were actually few revolutionaries among the socialists, and the theories of Karl Marx had by no means yet been substantiated by the course of events.

Even in a favorable situation, such as the parliamentary elections of 1912, the Social Democrats could muster, at best, only 110 out of a total of 400 representatives. They were certainly the strongest party (followed by the Catholic Center party with 90 representatives) but, because of the fact that the government was not responsible to the Reichstag in the real sense of the word, as has been stated, the chances that the Social Democrats would be able to exercise power in the Reichstag were definitely limited. On the other hand, the leadership of the Social Democrats had rid itself of revolutionary ideas and now sought to reach its goals by means of reform. In the political realm their reforming efforts were concentrated on the removal of the three-class voting system [2] in Prussia, which stood out in contrast to the universal franchise of the Empire. They also strove to establish a stronger parliamentary form of government, that is, to base its dependence upon the support of a majority. In these reforms the Social Democrats were backed by the middle class on the Left, but the Catholic Center party was not unanimous in its attitude toward these questions; the Center included not merely Catholic labor circles but also Catholic landholders and aristocrats who in these matters stood closer to the conservatives than to the Left. For a proper understanding of the political atmosphere one must always bear in mind that the circles which were really responsible for the government, the bureaucrats (especially the higher officials) and the Officers' Corps, were for the most part in favor of the existing order.

At the same time voices were raised on the Right in criticism of the total situation in the Reich. For example, the views of the historian Dietrich Schäfer. He, along with many like-minded associates, was in favor of a strengthening of German arms, because France had made substantially better use of its manpower for the army than had Germany. His basic position, however, did not differ radically from the prevailing feeling of the bourgeoisie. He said that the German nation, which seemed to have grown old, had instead recovered its youth since 1871. Yet even a man like Schäfer failed to recognize that the intrusion of the Germans into world affairs, with its fleet and its colonies, would inevitably create new opponents. In those days, and more often at a later time, it was said that Germany was being encircled. There never was an actual plan of this sort, but Germany gave the impression of being more aggressive than it actually was, and this encouraged the forming of alliances among those who felt themselves threatened.

This, then, was the Germany engulfed by war in August 1914. Germany did not want war. In fact, no country really wanted it in the way it came. But the errors Germany had made in its policy in the summer of 1914 seemed to have made war nearly inevitable, because Germany had given its ally, Austria-Hungary, practically a free hand to proceed against Serbia—and behind Serbia stood Russia, and France was allied with Russia. England had good grounds for intervening when the Germans invaded Belgium, which was regarded as neutral on the basis of old treaties. The Great War was on.

Chapter Two

The Germans and World War I

War! War in this highly civilized age! The generals had calculated on it, and, to a certain extent, each had made preparations for it in his own country. The politicians had reckoned with it as a remote possibility, but what did the German people know about war and what it would be like?

Germany had not known war since 1871. That had been a war in which casualties from disease had exceeded the losses inflicted by the enemy, and also, it had been a comparatively short war. By 1914 those who had fought in it were more than sixty years old. Of course the Germans knew that since then decisive steps had been taken to perfect weapons, and they were prepared for the fact that the troops would no longer go into battle in the old uniforms that were sometimes brilliant with colors. The new "field gray" uniforms were ready for the army—"our men in field gray!"

But who knew what war would really be like? A modern war on a grand scale had been carried on between Russia and Japan ten years before, but what would happen when the great powers of Europe clashed with one another? The Germans had fought a couple of colonial wars in Africa in the twentieth century, but nothing more.

For the moment there was no time to think about details. The masses had confidence in their leaders. Never again in

German history would such a firm trust and such a feeling of security prevail. Most of those who had been critical of German policy were convinced of the excellence of the military equipment and of the invincibility of the German army. Gigantic mobilization was under way, and volunteers were swarming to the army posts in such numbers that they could scarcely be controlled. There was general faith in the righteousness of the cause. Germany, it seemed, had been attacked by her enemies and by those who were envious of her.

There is much talk of the existence of "a frenzy of enthusiasm" in those first August days of 1914. That is a generalization and applies primarily to the big cities where the masses were aggregated; in smaller places people were calmer. Elly Heuss, the wife of Theodor Heuss,[1] reports from Heilbronn, "Here the mood is quite peaceful, deadly serious, silent." [2]

For people who remained at home war was to a certain extent the beginning of new experiences, but the really new and unprecedented befell the soldiers in the field. The original enthusiasm which had characterized the first few days remained with the troops for a time. Those staying behind had thronged around the departing soldiers; music had cheered them on; at all the railroad stations they had been greeted enthusiastically and had been well taken care of; and in the West they had crossed the Rhine. "Die Wacht am Rhein," even more so than "Deutschland, Deutschland über alles," came close to being made the national anthem. The official songs were the songs of the monarchy, especially "Heil Dir im Siegerkranz." Then came what was called "the baptism by fire." This was more or less severe, but not unexpected in mobile warfare in which men were not confined to one place but could move away from the dead and the wounded on the battlefield. There were of course some costly battles (the formations were still too close together as they moved forward against machine guns and against the very effective French field artillery). There were impressions for which people were not prepared inwardly, for which they could not be prepared. But the really difficult time did not come until static warfare and the battle for war material set in simultaneously, from 1916 onward. The entrenched positions lay opposite each other and were under constant fire as artillery and mortars began attacking them. As time went on withdrawal became impossible; the living were quartered with the dead and the wounded, and terrors multiplied. Verdun and the Somme— these were the first symbols of horror for the Germans.

All the troops were not engaged in these strategic battles; many units spent the entire period of the war in a comparatively peaceful area, but it was at the front that the experiences of the war imprinted themselves on the mind. Here are some quotations from early letters from the front: "The talk about things has stopped, in this heat all ideals are consumed, or they become harder than steel and diamonds." [3]

"I have learned out here that one must accept life, each of course in his own way." [4]

"You smoke, you converse, you fire. Can you believe that a person who has never violated the established practices of the social order lies here in ambush waiting to kill?" [5] Another writes: "My God, that looked awful. How often I wished for war, but such scenes can never be forgotten—that is too much." [6] These are letters from the first four weeks. I have not selected anything from the numerous passages that speak of victory and of the righteousness of the cause, because it is the individual who is confronted by the war. The horrifying things were having their effect, but there is also the statement about ideals: only that which is genuine is preserved. Many men who wrote nothing about patriotism saw meaning in this. But soon the general tone became more serious, at least among those who had long been engaged in battle. It became more difficult to impart to those at home (a peacetime generation) any conception of what was being experienced. "You loved ones have no idea what war means," and "from your letters one can see how we who are out here have changed." [7] Both of these are from the end of 1914. And soon came the question, "Should things at home remain the same after the war as before?" And ever and again complaints about the newspapers at home, especially those that were coloring their dispatches in rosy hue. Such complaints were also to be heard at home, among people who had imagination and conscience. Soon Elly Heuss was writing about the sensationalism and the false tone of the press, she longed for the fine, elevated mood of the first weeks of the war.[8]

The letters from the front were still full of praise for life, because those who had survived danger felt it to be especially beautiful. And soon the question was asked, "Will the home front hold out too?" It was said of the soldiers in 1916, "When they take off their uniforms and do not receive what they can easily demand, they will take it somehow, and then they will be driven into the arms of the International." [9] How glad the soldiers were that the people at home did not have to witness the "devastation and the terrible misery" of the war.

Among the letters of the first few war years those of the painter Franz Marc stand out. Marc was rarely engaged in heavy fighting, but he had observed much before he fell in March 1916. "The socialists are getting a stranglehold on 'those in power.' What is happening today will never be forgotten by the nations. The ground is being prepared today for the most impressive movement of the fourth estate." [10] Exalting letters are especially numerous in the collection, *Kriegsbriefe Gefallener Studenten* [War Letters of Students Killed in Action]. As might be expected, more idealism is found here than in the letters of the average soldier: "It seems to me that we who have stood before the enemy are freed from everything that otherwise bound us, we are completely free, death does not dare sever connections in too painful a fashion." [11]

It is difficult to reduce to uniformity the abundant correspondence that has come down to us. The letters selected are naturally one-sided, usually the volumes have been published for the express purpose of glorifying the heroism of soldiers and of establishing a memorial to them. It is surprising to note in this connection that popular patriotism, such as thoughts on "heroism," is almost completely absent from these letters. The breach between the army and the home front, which continued to have its effect later on, in a different form, is first seen here. This did, however, not become completely clear until the second half of the war.

On the western front, at least at the focal points, more endurance was demanded of the German soldier from 1916 on, than of Germany's allies or enemies. For weeks at a time the German soldier would lie in a position that was being hammered at by hostile artillery; he had hardly any nourishment, had received no relief for a long time, and was cut off from the hope of ever escaping from this inferno. And all around him his comrades were dying—anyone who managed to survive was a changed man. These were the war experiences that caused the most serious aftereffects.

The way was also being prepared for another conflict: official patriotism clung, even after the war, to the events of the autumn of 1914, especially to the battle of Langemark, Flanders. In that engagement poorly trained German volunteers had been sent against British professional soldiers. The Germans suffered tremendous casualties, but they charged, as the army report stated, "with the German national anthem on their lips." From a military viewpoint this sacrifice of men was madness. It proved that the war leadership was in the grip of irresponsible optimism. But it also became the symbol of the self-sacrifice that characterized the young generation of Germans who in 1914 went from their comfortable life directly into battle. Later this symbol was often used with justification, but it was also misused. The even more heroically endured suffering and perseverance in the West during the second half of the war did not find such a clear symbol, but had a more decided aftereffect upon those who had experienced it. In some it led to a hatred of all patriotic phrases, in others, to a fundamental resistance to war.

But now let us turn to the people who had stayed at home. Small groups had been against the war, against any war regardless of its cause, from the beginning. They had no influence upon the people as a whole. Yet let us cite these lines written by Franz Werfel in August of 1914: "God's eyes fill with tears at any kindness, and a little love pervades the whole system, but woe to thee, chaotic time, woe to the abominable stream of idle talk!" [12] Yet such moods remained esoteric.

After the first few weeks everyday life at home became harder. It grew even more severe when the consequences of the enemy blockade became apparent. Privations, just like battles on the front, could be borne if they lasted a short time and if an end was in sight. But they became unbearable when the months stretched out, when hardships increased, and when no end was in sight. The privations began with a shortage of necessities; women, whose husbands were in the field, could hardly nourish their children. The winter of 1916–17 was especially severe, the bread in the cities was practically inedible; it was a winter of turnips and of beets.

At the same time people were without any real morale-building leadership. The slogan, "We have taken up arms in our own defense," could not be maintained indefinitely, especially since not everyone agreed about the aims of the war. Soon an open quarrel arose over this question. The rightist circles, ignoring the military prospects, set their aims high: Belgium, which had been attacked by Germany in 1914, although its neutrality had been guaranteed by treaties, should be kept as a dependency by Germany. There is no doubt that Germany, if it had been victorious, would have imposed severe conditions on its enemies—this must be kept in mind when the Treaty of Versailles is discussed. The moderate circles were more realistic at this point, but their chief argument—in itself correct—that Germany could not win the war in the face of the superiority of the Allies could not be openly expressed without crippling the will of the people to continue fighting.

However, something else proved to be more damaging to the German cause. The Empire, whose political system appeared to handle the war preparations extremely well, was actually less capable of waging modern warfare than the democratic states of the enemy in the West whose system was so different in its make-up.

In addition to the controversy over the war's aims, a dispute over whether or not to use unrestricted submarine warfare was in progress. (This method of conducting war meant that commercial ships could be attacked without warning once a prohibited area had been announced.) [13] The quarrel had disastrous effects upon the people. The rightist advocates of this form of warfare misjudged the technical problems involved as well as the significance of such an action. Never before in all Prussian-German history has such rashness prevailed as in the navy's calculation of what chances of success their plans had. Equal rashness was shown when the question whether it would make any difference if the United States of America entered the war on the enemy's side was discussed. These misconceptions rested partly upon the anti-England complex encouraged by Admiral Tirpitz. They also reveal how little the people in imperial Germany, which boasted of the most advanced scientific techniques in the world, knew or wanted to know about the elementary aspects of life in other countries.

In the last winter of the war (1917–18) the German horizon once more glowed with a misleading light. Russia had collapsed. The Bolsheviks had been forced to make peace. Germany had better possibilities of getting food and oil from the East and could now concentrate upon the struggle in the West. It is uncanny, when one reads about it today, how generally the Americans, the new adversaries in the West, were underestimated. The submarines had never succeeded in seriously interrupting the vast transport of American troops to Europe.

Then came 1918, the year of sudden change and of collapse. It began with the last great German offensive against the French and the English, which, however, came too late: "More than four years of war are a little too much for the soul," read one letter from the field.[14] And by October 1918: "It was terrible tonight, and it is a wonder that men hold out. But it is pitiful to hear them moan because they can hardly hold out much longer. One does not dare think about it." [15]

"One does not dare think about it." Heavy sorrows weighed upon nearly all segments of German society in those fall days. One must not believe, in view of the subsequent revolution, that the majority of the socialists were happy over the bad military situation. Only a small group of them worked toward revolution without considering the danger involved as far as international affairs were concerned. In 1917 minor naval mutinies had taken place, which, however, had less political background than the courts-martial had at that time assumed. They had been occasioned by incontrovertible abuses that existed on the big ships whose crews had been doomed to inactivity. Of more serious consequence were the strikes of January 1918, but these were soon settled, with the help of the leaders of the Social Democrats.

In England there were more strikes during the war than there were in Germany, and the mutinies of the French frontline troops in 1917 were much more serious than those that occurred in Germany before the end of October 1918. Neither the strikes nor the insignificant mutiny of the fleet in 1917 had any considerable influence upon the course of the war.

At the end of September 1918, after the failure of the offensive, Erich von Ludendorff [16] suddenly lost his nerve and called upon the government to ask the enemy for an armistice. However, the administration was just being re-formed, and for the first time in German history a parliamentary form of government was being set up—a government that was set up with the active participation of the parties, and whose ministers were responsible to the Reichstag. This government was under the leadership of the new chancellor, Prince Max von Baden, a man who made every effort to salvage whatever could be saved from the hopeless situation.

At this point we must look back to the development of internal politics in Germany during the war. That is, to what was apparent to the people.

In those August days of 1914 all internal strife appeared to have ceased. The Kaiser cried: "I know no parties anymore, I know only Germans!" The Reichstag, which had been elected in 1912, was convened at the beginning of the war and continued in office throughout the war. The Social Democrats were the strongest party in the Reichstag, as we have already noted. At the beginning they unanimously approved the war loans, in spite of some internal opposition—an action regarded as incorrect by socialists abroad.

Matters at home and military matters at the front were considered in the same light: the war was expected to be a short one, and, therefore, a political truce was declared. But the war dragged on, the soldiers who marched out in August and who hoped to be home by Christmas were to return only after four, and many of them after five, Christmases—that is, those who were still alive.

I have spoken briefly about the inner structure of the Empire. A dangerous political injustice existed within the Empire that could become an issue in time of war. The army got its men by conscription—everyone had to be prepared to sacrifice his life. In Prussia, the largest state of the Empire, the three-class voting system prevailed. According to this system the political voting power of an individual was determined by his taxes, that is, according to his income and his property. The abolition of the three-class voting system had been one of the goals of the leftists before the war. During the war this cause was more justifiable than ever before—because of universal conscription—but on the other hand it is understandable that for the time being internal political questions were forced into the background. "Truce!" was the patriotic cry.

But this truce was being broken from two different sides. For one thing, the dispute over the war aims could no longer be smothered; how should the peace treaty look? The first discussions concerning the war aims took place in the flush of the early German victories, and were inspired by the fact that the German armies were for the most part fighting on enemy soil; even the Russians had been repulsed after their invasion of East Prussia (at Tannenberg by Hindenburg and Ludendorff).[17] Nearly the whole of Belgium had been subjugated. Even after the battle of the Marne the German army stood deep in north-eastern France. This misleading picture of the true course of the struggle was the reason why the rightists, as I have pointed out, demanded large annexations of territory. That this contradicted the thesis that Germany had taken up arms only in its own defense is certain, but it was justified by the claim that the door would thus be barred against any similar future attacks upon Germany. The masses were hardly interested in this question, but they would probably have looked upon the securing of German holdings as evidence of a successful conclusion of the war—precisely because of the thesis that Germany had been attacked.

The other special area of internal discussion were the Social Democrats.[18] After 1915 the leftist wing of the party refused to finance the war and withheld approval of further war loans. Later on, the question of the voting system in Prussia was taken up. The counterargument of the royal Prussian government (government of the Reich) was that during the war no internal controversies should be fought out. The conservatives, especially, opposed any change in the franchise. Even the proposal to give a vote to everyone who had participated in the war, for example to the combat veterans, was rejected. The intention had been to give a larger vote to those in the low-income bracket by counting the sacrifice which they had been called upon to make for Germany, in addition to or instead of the amount paid in taxes. This is the historic offense of the conservative forces in Prussia—of the nobility, of the land-owners, of the industrialists, and also of the upper middle class. The English conservatives have always been more flexi-ble and more realistic when confronted by such situations. The conservatives in the Prussian Landtag suffered from an obstinate leadership, who believed that a long war could be waged under the system of compulsory military service with-out giving those conscripts who belonged to the lower classes adequate political rights. Although there were some other causes, the old order broke up as a result of this inflexibility.[19]

It is still an open question, as those who are interested in political and historical matters most probably have observed, to what extent the western parliamentary system, whether in the English or in the French form, was and is transferable to Germany. When one expresses such an opinion—seldom dis-cussed in Germany today—one must add that the purely nega-tive position taken during World War I was certainly wrong. This must be emphasized all the more because the older Ger-man history books, which for the most part were written by men coming from the conservative ranks of that day, are one-sided. And because, in contrast, the political community today answers the question by saying that a western parliamentary form should simply have been accepted. They assume that at that time it would have been possible simply to accept it. This answer is not right either, because the broad social prerequi-sites for a simple acceptance were lacking. Though social pat-terns and political patterns are known to affect each other, time is needed for that to come about; political patterns that do not correspond to the social patterns are created only with considerable difficulty.[20]

That is my opinion. I must state it in advance, as I shall

now cite certain of Max Weber's utterances and comment upon them. Max Weber, about whom you may read in the publication of Karl Jaspers,[21] in the biography by his widow, Marianne Weber, and in an introduction by Theodor Heuss,[22] was professor of national economics in Heidelberg from the year 1897. He gave up his academic chair on account of illness but was still a resident of Heidelberg and was very active there until he was called to the University of Munich in 1919, where he died the following year. He was a man of great comprehensive intellect but is of interest to us here only for his political views. As a student he had belonged to a Heidelberg fraternity, had become a reserve officer, and was, therefore, according to the opinion of the times, a member of the best circles. Later he changed his views and became sharply critical of the accepted principles of education, of the dueling practices of the students,[23] and of the Reserve Officers' Corps. But he was always a devoted patriot, and not a man who looked on political questions with cold reason only. He could sympathize with nationalistic passion. He had, however, become a liberal and strove ardently to give the German people a social and political constitution that was democratic and based on the parliamentary system in the western sense.

From the beginning of the war he appraised the German military position soberly, even skeptically. In contrast to many other German academic men, he was acquainted with the outside world and had also been in America—which for that time was a rarity, at least among intellectuals. He was also well versed in the English political system and knew the vigor that is to be found in English political life. He indulged in no illusions but looked upon the war as a consequence of the founding of the German Reich: "If we didn't want to run the risk of fighting this war, then we should have abstained from founding the Reich, and we could have continued to exist as a nation of small states." [24] The war must not, as Weber said, be carried on "for the purpose of changing the map, or for economic profit." He was enraged when many noncombatants who remained at home clamored for large annexations. Every opportunity for attaining a peace restoring the status quo should be seized upon. Here, according to Weber, lay the real tragedy of the war. The great successes of the early period (which, when seen in retrospect, were nothing more than illusionary victories) merely befogged the political judgment of many Germans, which in any case was not altogether clear. Big demands were being planned in anticipation of peace, which only strengthened the determination on the part of the adversaries to continue the war. Moreover, the French from the very beginning had their own territorial ambitions; they wanted Alsace and that part of Lorraine that had fallen to the Reich in 1871. They had never really accepted this cession of territory. Seen as a whole, the situation was somewhat as follows: If Germany could retain in Europe its status as of 1914, it would win this war in the same sense that Frederick the Great had won the Seven Years War.[25]

Many others understood the situation at that time, but few saw it so clearly as Weber. At first he had called the war "great and wonderful." He thought it great that a people "who live in the midst of a refined culture, could nevertheless be a match for the horrors of war away from home (which is no feat for a Senegal negro). . . . That is mankind at its best—and this must not be overlooked—in spite of the imposition of unpleasant activities. This experience remains—whatever the outcome may be." [26] But then as early as the end of 1915, in connection with a visit to Brussels, he wrote: "The liberally educated are opposed to the annexation [of Belgium]. But such views have no influence at the present time. Every victory removes us further from peace, that is the peculiar thing about the situation." [27] And then he spoke out concerning the plan for colonizing Courland. "Mere fantasies, as if we were alone in the world!" [28]

Alone in the world! The discussion about the war aims in

the Reichstag in the summer of 1917 resulted in a "peace resolution" of the majority, which looked forward to a "peace with understanding," without annexations. In opposition to this, the party of the Fatherland was founded in September, whose opinion it was that every renunciation of annexations made in advance, every declaration of a peace with understanding, would be looked upon by Germany's enemies as signs of weakness. This argument must be taken quite seriously, even if we today have historical perspective and know what Germany's situation at that time really was, and, therefore, regard all plans for annexation a tragic political error.

The controversy about war aims and the problem of political reform at home occupied Max Weber's thoughts continually. The fate of Germany depended upon the solution of such problems as much as on the military outcome of the war. The stage was being set for what was to come later—right down to the present day. It is for this reason that I tarry so long on this point.

You will recall that the question was often asked in letters written during the war: "Should things at home remain the same after the war as before?" The combat veterans in general, regardless of their individual political views, were of one mind in this: Much would have to be different. At any rate those who had fought for Germany should have something to say—not only those who had stayed at home and who had been permitted by fate to play politics or to manage business or to make profits out of war.[29] To this must be added other voices, also of soldiers. These belonged politically to the far Right and called for a reorganization of the political and social order. Common soldiers were among them, and so were the lieutenants who in the second half of the war virtually assumed command of the smaller units, when the regular officers had been killed or had been promoted to higher positions of leadership or had been transferred to headquarters. The social makeup of the imperial army was, however, not flexible

enough to grant to reserve officers who participated in the war
the same opportunities for promotion as were available to
regular officers under similar circumstances.

It is stirring to note how Max Weber cautioned against the
declaration of unrestricted submarine warfare by putting forward theories that later proved to be justified, whereas the
navy was guilty of miscalculations in both political and military matters.

Weber complained about the consequences of the Bismarck
era: "The bureaucratic spirit ruled where another, namely the
guiding spirit of the politician, should have ruled." Later in
the war he said: "We are wearing an iron ring around our
hearts." [30] He became quieter and regretted that he did not
know what was going on. To the very end he remained a
devotee of the monarchy, that is, of a monarchy limited by
parliament. But he knew that the German Reichstag, because
of its past, had pursued a policy that was essentially negative
and was, therefore, now well prepared.[31]

The historian, Friedrich Meinecke,[32] had convictions similar to those of Weber. Here is one more example, "The reform
of the voting system," he wrote at the beginning of 1918, "is in
the present situation for us Centrists nothing less than . . . a
powerful means to keep the state and the Fatherland . . . as
strong and as capable of defense as possible, both in the turbu-
lent time of the World War and in . . . the future." Generally speaking, he was more theoretical than Weber and was
bound more firmly to tradition. When, however, in October
1918, under the pressure of the situation and in the face of the
demands of President Wilson, a parliamentary government
was introduced into Germany, he too wrote: "Everything now
depends upon our recognizing and supporting the new democratic order of our Fatherland." [33]

From the end of September on, when Ludendorff forced the
new government to make an offer of armistice, things began to
move so rapidly that the German people could not recover

quickly, indeed, never have recovered from the onslaught of misfortunes that befell Germany. It must be borne in mind that up to July 1918 the German offensives were being pushed forward in the West, and well into August the official reports had been completely reassuring. Peace had been made with the revolutionaries in Russia; the pressure from the East appeared to have let up. Then came the collapse of Bulgaria, and among the other allies Turkey was the next to make an armistice with the enemy, and at the end of October Austria-Hungary gave up the fight. This all happened within a few weeks—a sudden change from assurance of victory to the realization that the war was lost. And just as this realization began slowly to sink in, the mutiny of the German fleet, the prelude to revolution, began at the end of October.

During the last weeks of the war the Prussian representatives in the Landtag and the upper house agreed to the abolition of the three-class voting system. But it was too late, and the assent went almost unnoticed in the whirlpool of events. Germany did not lose the war because of the three-class voting system in Prussia, but those who opposed its abolition demonstrated that they did not understand that a popular war cannot be waged unless every individual citizen, if he has the right and the duty to sacrifice his life, also should be able to exercise the political rights which correspond to this sacrifice. I have previously mentioned the arguments against the change; they are not conclusive. The representatives of the old Prussian powers had shown that they no longer understood the times, and they had merely underlined this fact by yielding before the monarchy came to an end—when it was ineffective and too late.

Chapter Three

Revolution, Armistice,
and Versailles

On October 29, 1918, a mutiny began on board the ships of the imperial fleet. The naval leaders had wanted to make a thrust into the English Channel with the fleet. It is not for us to discuss the pros and cons of this decision—the fact is, many seamen had had enough of fighting. The mutiny spread from Wilhelmshaven to other naval bases; Kiel was seized on November 4th. The German warflag, to which had been dedicated the much chanted flag song, "Proudly the Flag Waves, the Black-White-and-Red, on the Mast of our Ship," was hauled down and the red flag was hoisted.[1] It came to light that on the big ships the relationship between officers and members of the crew was not good.

How did the officers behave during this mutiny? Three officers of the imperial navy fell defending the flag: they were the commander and two officers of the battleship *König*. The revolution-minded sailors now began to stream to the land in special trains (frequently they were men who had never been to sea). The Republic was proclaimed in Munich on November 7th and in Berlin on November 9th. At the end of October the Kaiser had already set out for the army headquarters at Spa, in Belgium. Many believed that the Kaiser was responsible for the continuation of the war. The government urged William II to abdicate. He crossed the proximate border of Holland, and placed himself under the protection of the Netherlands.[2]

When I was young, people in middle-class rightist groups often recited a poem of the nineteenth century: "What is gone will not return, but if it went down brilliantly, its glory will shine for a long time." [3] To make such a claim for the monarchy would have been a pious illusion; for it did not decline brilliantly, if one considers how few were the hands raised in its defense and how the commander in chief conducted himself. But it did go down brilliantly, if one considers the heroic and self-sacrificing struggle, through long years, of the German troops in all theaters of war. In the colony of German East Africa, that is, in the neighboring Portuguese colony, a small contingent under Lettow-Vorbeck held out until the news of the armistice came, but otherwise all overseas possessions of the Empire had been lost in 1914 or in 1915.

On a Sunday, the 10th of November, the Germans found out from extra editions (at that time newspapers were hawked and the headlines loudly proclaimed—the quickest means of imparting news through the streets) the conditions under which the armistice was to be granted. The terms were equivalent to capitulation.

General Erich von Ludendorff had been replaced by General Wilhelm Groener [4] toward the end of October, but there is no reason to believe that Ludendorff would have proposed anything different. At the most he might have refused to remain in office afterwards, but then he had already departed.[5]

What did the German people think of revolution and armistice? It is difficult to give an overall answer. What was the relationship between the military defeat and the revolution? It should be established, in contradiction to what the opponents of the republic and especially the National Socialists claimed, that not even the majority of those socialists (with a few exceptions), who had previously hoped for the abolition of the monarchy, rejoiced loudly over the revolution in the face of military defeat. The word "freedom" tasted bitter under the conditions of the armistice. When the last imperial chancellor, Prince Max von Baden, turned over the government to the leader of the administration appointed by the revolutionaries, the Prince said: "Mr. Ebert, I lay the German Empire upon your heart." Ebert replied, "I lost two sons for this Empire."

Indeed, Philipp Scheidemann,[6] who proclaimed the republic in Berlin, had said: "The German people were victorious all along the line," but he had said that in order to take the wind out of the sails of the radicals, the Spartacists.[7] However, among the ranks of the radicals, and especially among literary men with leanings to the Left, hardly any trace was to be found of Ebert's way of thinking. The physical needs of the Fatherland were forgotten for the time being in the jubilation over the new freedom, which, however, was also associated with humiliations suffered in international politics.

Let us look clearly for a moment at what had happened to the German people between August 1914 and November 1918, that is, in little over four years, and compare this period with a similar one in our own lives. During the first days of August 1914 the church bells rang; the people, with the exception of a few who hardly expressed themselves, were inspired with the task of defending the Fatherland, which they believed had been attacked. Hardly more than four years later two million had died in battle. The people were perplexed—the enemies, whom they had hoped to overcome in 1914, had triumphed. Only four years had passed, but for the Germans the world had changed. The German citizens went about their daily business miserably underfed and wretchedly clothed; they had given up their gold for the Fatherland, their sons had been killed or were prisoners of war, and those who had returned home were terribly changed.

The most crucial thing in all this was not, however, the

outward change—the change from the clean streets and the well-kept homes of the summer of 1914, to the shabby streets on which half-starved children and poorly dressed adults moved about in November 1918—but the inner change. Even most of the socialists in 1914, though they had wanted to reform it, had taken the government and its strength and security completely for granted. The values in which the preponderant majority of the German people had believed in 1914, naturally with slight differences, were now shaken. If one can speak of the self-assurance of a people, then this self-assurance of the Germans was now endangered. The visible wounds to the country itself were few. There had been only a limited amount of bombing, and only the cities in the Rhine territory had been devastated. In the West, the enemy occupied only the important region west of the Rhine. But in the German East the situation was more gruesome, especially on the borders of Poland. Here survivors from old units and from the German volunteer corps, or Freikorps,[8] were constantly defending themselves against the Poles who were pressing ahead.

For the Germans the summer of 1919 was darkened by various troubles. There was first of all, the question of the peace treaty. Just as the terms of the armistice had been formulated so that Germany could not revoke them and continue fighting, so the terms of the peace treaty were meant to render Germany harmless for the future—such was the will of the victors, for according to their opinion, Germany was guilty of causing the war.

Many people believe that Germany began to go astray after the signing of the Treaty of Versailles, and that the treaty was solely responsible for the emergence of radical nationalism in the style of Hitler. This is a false oversimplification, and a dangerous one.

The Treaty of Versailles was severe, but it was no more severe than the peace treaty the German rightists had planned for the enemy in the event of victory, and not so severe as the one the victorious Germans had inflicted upon the Russians in the winter of 1917–18 (especially if the Russian Empire is considered as a unit, as it naturally was by the Russians).[9] But peace was encumbered by the demand of the Allies that the Germans acknowledge the German and Austro-Hungarian war guilt and extradite the so-called war criminals. These were the "paragraphs of insult" that kindled the defiance of many Germans. Whatever has been said since about the terms of the peace treaty to exonerate the Allies is wrong. Especially if it is said that the admission of guilt was merely to have been the prerequisite for the payment of reparations. Obviously, there were people on both sides who had conducted the war in an inhuman fashion. That only the defeated side should have to turn in its so-called war criminals and allow the victorious side to punish them was foolhardy, and combined principles of law with the mere demands of power.

In this summer of 1919 a vehement discussion arose over the question of whether the peace conditions of the Allies were to be accepted or not. This discussion was a heavy blow to the new state. In January 1919 a National Assembly, whose task it was to frame a constitution, had been elected on the basis of the universal and equal voting privilege. The strongest party in this first parliament of the republic was that of the Social Democrats, who had 165 of a total of 423 seats. From these a radical leftist group now split off and became the Independent Social Democratic party, with 22 seats. The Communist party as an electoral group did not exist. On the other hand, it became apparent that the majority of the German people did not favor socialism. The middle-class parties had the majority; among them were the old conservatives and related groups which had joined them, but these had only 44 seats. On account of the continual agitations in Berlin, the National Assembly convened in Weimar. There it held its long discussions and there, in August, it brought forth the new Constitution, hence the name "Weimar Republic."

The National Assembly chose as its first president the former chairman of the People's Commission, Friedrich Ebert,[10] who came from Heidelberg and now lies buried there. Ebert was a true statesman. He was the personification of the best forces of the Social Democrats—the party of the opposition that, at last, had assumed the responsibility of government—a man who represented the new republic with firm dignity. Every attempt of the radical leftists to form a revolutionary minority government against the will of the majority of the people had been rendered impossible through the existence of the National Assembly. Through it the reign of workers and soldiers councils of the winter also came to an end. But the stability of the new republic's power depended mainly upon the building of a new army.

Though most of the combat units had returned to Germany in good order (one last organizational accomplishment of the old army), most of the units broke up quickly, once they were back, because the soldiers wanted to go home; Christmas was coming. Some units, old companies, mostly those stationed in the East, remained behind. Together with these were the Freikorps (sometimes old troop fragments were their nuclei), who had been formed for the protection of the boundaries in the East and for the preservation of internal order. The strength of these Freikorps depended upon their leaders. At that time, therefore, the importance of the officer had further increased because the army no longer had a commander in chief and was not supported by statutory laws. Considering what had occurred during the revolution, this is a paradox.

On November 10, 1918, the day the terms of the armistice had been announced, Ebert had conferred with General Groener at the supreme army command and had commissioned Hindenburg to lead the troops back home. It was now a question of raising a new army. The obvious choice was an officer from Württemberg. Destined to become the last Prussian minister of war, Walter Reinhardt was a man who had practically alone repulsed the power of the soldiers councils in tenacious negotiations and had restored the power of command to the officers. Reinhardt was the creator of the Reichswehr, as the army of the republic was called.

One must bear clearly in mind that the people, with few exceptions, were tired of bearing arms, that especially the officers were shaken by the revolution and by the Kaiser's flight to Holland, and that many elements in the Social Democratic party (which was now in the forefront of things) could not look kindly upon the thought of any army that gave explicit power of command to its officers. It was fortunate, therefore, that Gustave Noske,[11] the former reporter on defense matters of the Social Democratic party in the old Reichstag, now became minister of defense and supported Reinhardt; Ebert and some other Social Democratic leaders agreed with Noske. Thus it was not really a broad foundation, but rather a narrow ledge, upon which the Weimar Republic was built, and the officers for the most part felt little sympathy for it.

Into this situation came the vehement debate over the acceptance of the peace treaty. In June 1919 the conditions of the treaty were made public and, at first, all parties rejected them, but then came countercurrents; there was widespread fear, and rightly so, that all of Germany would be occupied by the enemy. The French troops along the Rhine were openly supporting every endeavor by separatists to set up Rhine states servile to French authority. (Such attempts were repeated, on a lesser scale, after 1945.) The newly formed government concentrated its last efforts at resistance on an attempt to exclude at least the war-guilt clauses and the articles on the war criminals from the treaty. But again the opponents, who permitted only written negotiations, did not yield.

Especially petty and eager for vengeance was the Frenchman, Georges Clemenceau. But also David Lloyd George, the representative of England, swung over only slowly to the view that traditional English policy required, that no state (in this

instance, France) should become too powerful on the conti-
nent. Wilson, the American president, to whose Fourteen
Points the German government had appealed when asking for
an armistice (the Fourteen Points had also been rejected by
the Germans when they were first announced) was repelled at
the peace conference. Besides, he, as well as nearly all American politicians of the old school and, as yet, many of the new
school, understood too little about Europe.

The cession of Alsace-Lorraine had been expected. Even in
Alsace a referendum at that time would have found few resi-
dents in favor of continuing connections with Germany.
Poland received nearly all of West Prussia, without a referendum being held there, and so the Corridor between the main
part of Germany and East Prussia was established. In one part
of East Prussia and Upper Silesia referendums were to be held
to determine whether the population wished to become part of
Poland or wished to remain with Germany. Similarly, a referendum was to be held on the Danish frontier. The Saar territory was to be administered for fifteen years by the League of
Nations, which was being created.

A majority had gradually formed in the National Assembly
that favored signing the treaty even though the victors rejected the proviso against the statement of war guilt and the
surrendering of war criminals. So the treaty was signed in the
Hall of Mirrors in the palace at Versailles, where the German
Empire had been founded in 1871.

Seen objectively, the Treaty of Versailles—the "Versailler
Diktat" as it was called—was not the cause of National Socialism. But there can be no doubt that it had a fateful impact on
the German consciousness. A battle was also raging over the
assertion of the Allies that the sole responsibility for the war
lay with Germany and Austria-Hungary. A great wave of ob-
jection arose against this in Germany, in the form of propaganda, and, of course, also led to a biased attitude. It is certainly true that, even though German mistakes helped cause

the war, the imperial German government did not work toward a war; did not want war. Austria-Hungary is more blameworthy; it made war inevitable by its action against Serbia in July 1914, though among the enemy countries, Russia and France were certainly also to blame.[12]

For the internal political development in Germany, placing the responsibility for the collapse was more important. Most of the German socialists even began to see that the imperial government had not wanted war. As far as the collapse itself was concerned, rightist circles soon after the armistice conceived the idea of the "stab in the back," which today is called the "legend of the stab in the back." Here lies one of the principal roots of the trouble and, therefore, I must speak of this in somewhat greater detail.[13]

"Stab in the back" has something of the Siegfried image in it. The hero (in this case, the army) fights against an opponent and is brought down in the struggle by a stab in the back. Applied to 1918 the term means that the German army was engaged in battle when the socialists and the pacifists delivered the stab in the back; moreover, the German army was fighting a promising battle, and only this "stab in the back" prevented it from continuing to fight. There was a narrower and a broader interpretation of this idea. The narrower one claimed that the revolution of 1918 rendered a German victory or at least an honorable peace treaty impossible. The broader one claimed that significant forces had weakened, and even sabotaged, German war efforts from the beginning—otherwise Germany would have won the war.

In this connection we must take into consideration that in modern warfare a single unit may still consider itself undefeated, even if the war has been lost. To be specific: the withdrawing German troops, in Belgium and in northern France in 1918, felt betrayed by those at the home front who plundered supply trains and held up ammunition trains. It is easy to understand that the leader of such a unit, returning home at the head of his contingent some weeks later, was hardly concerned about the outcome of the war in general. And then the cares of everyday life in Germany at the end of 1918 began, and left no time for a calm review of past events.

Actually, Germany had lost the war at the time when the mutiny broke out at the end of October. The mutiny was not the cause of the defeat—it was one of its symptoms.[14]

What, then, can be said of the broader interpretation of the "stab in the back"? It does not have any justification either. Strikes did not interfere with the war effort in Germany any more than they did in other countries, and the minor mutinies of 1917 had no military significance. The radical underground propaganda against the war was not effective until the summer of 1918, when the failure of the offensive in the West had already become apparent. The war had already been lost at that time. Then Bulgaria had capitulated. Ludendorff himself had explained that without Rumanian oil, which was now no longer available, the war could not be carried on.[15] And then came the collapse of Austria. Germany, retreating in the West, was faced with the problem of having to defend a new front in the Southeast, and more important still—the Americans had just brought part of their fresh troops to Europe. The German western front would have crumbled in the spring of 1919, at the very latest.

Therefore, the idea of the "stab in the back," upon which Hitler constructed his historical image, is a legend. Yet it had some foundation in fact. Until the summer of 1918 the German troops had been deep in enemy territory, and this had prevented the people, even their leaders, from understanding the actual situation. After that everything went so rapidly that quiet reflection was no longer possible.

Soon, however, the legend of the "stab in the back" was used in political battles—mostly by people who had never been at the front. Even though the achievements of the German army, from 1914 to 1918, had been great, they did not affect the outcome of a war that from the beginning had been rather hopeless. For a long time the German people had not been aware of the real situation; when the sudden realization came, the German middle class, at any rate, never really assimilated it.

I myself am, perhaps, not the worst witness in this matter, since I grew up in the midst of this atmosphere. In our high school in Stuttgart, as, indeed, in most of the secondary schools in Germany after 1918, a noticeable rightist trend prevailed, which most of the teachers followed, at least those who spoke to us about politics. We believed that it was the "stab in the back" alone that had prevented a German victory; we had one Pan-German history teacher who defended this worst form of the legend. We were convinced that one could be patriotic only on the rightist side. We repeated the stupid jokes, which were then circulating among the middle class, about President Ebert and his wife, and which were supposed to prove their unworthiness. In fact, the Eberts succeeded, with quiet dignity, in regaining sympathy for Germany under the most trying conditions—in a world in which public opinion was dominated by Germany's wartime enemies. About this, however, we heard nothing, and we read nothing about it in our rightist middle-class press. We did not know what the actual situation of the war had been in 1918; we were taught to hate the French and the British and to despise the Americans. We were pressed into a form that had become empty. We did not see that the socialist workers had also sacrificed their blood for Germany—for a country that had never really given them a chance.[16] We were not meant to suspect that the leading classes of imperial Germany had made serious mistakes, and that these had jeopardized the victory (if victory had ever been a possibility) as much as the trend to the Left had. We were brought up for a world that no longer existed, and we took up nationalistic slogans, while the republic of which we were making fun was trying to pull the wagon out of the mud.

After graduation many of our class joined the "black army." [17] It was at this point that I, a student and a student-apprentice in Stuttgart, broke through this form and saw how wrong we were. Thus, at eighteen, I became immune to the allurements of Hitlerism and could observe the rise of the Weimar Republic with keen interest.

But in another respect we too were children of the revolution. World War I had destroyed what had been an accepted fact of life—the authority of the German school (even though the school, and more so the middle-class environment, influenced our political outlook), and the control that the school masters—and to a certain extent the older generation as a whole—had over our lives went with it. This was not felt so much as after 1945, but it was, nevertheless, felt strongly enough. Also in question were the traditional values of the German educational system, the classical education, according to which French was the only modern foreign language still being taught in most of Germany, and then often enough as a dead language. Now it began to dawn upon many of the older teachers in Germany that English had become an indispensable language, and that the future in the West belonged to the Anglo-Saxon world.

The repression of classical education within the overall educational framework has damaged the educational system of Germany. Hitler continued this repression, just as he degraded anything intellectual. Unfortunately not enough has been done since 1945 to repair this damage. If I seem particularly to emphasize the value of a classical education, it is, of course, a subjective viewpoint, especially in such a brief presentation. But I can only confirm the fact that in discussions held at the University of Heidelberg after 1945, especially the students of medicine and of natural science expressed the viewpoint that humanistic studies provide the best foundation for an academic education. Admittedly, they meant a humanistic high school that was free from many superficialities but did have philologists able to explain the eternal values of the ancient world to the students without ignoring or scorning what came after it.

The passions aroused in the winter of 1918–19 did not get a chance to subside. They were, however, forced into the background, for a time, in the period that followed. Today people realize that, in a historical sense, the peace treaty could not have been rejected because the unity of Germany would then have been endangered. But at that time there were men, such as Walter Reinhardt, who pleaded for its rejection even though they felt no sympathy for the national slogans. Soon, from another side, there were agitations against those who had to sign the armistice and the peace treaty—the representatives of the Catholic Center, Matthias Erzberger and Bell, and the Social Democrat, Hermann Müller. This "national" agitation against those in favor of the republic marked the most disgraceful chapter in recent German history and led to the treacherous assassination of Erzberger and Rathenau and then directly to the advent of Hitler. It was so ignominious because it also took hold of solid middle-class circles, of people who prided themselves upon their honor and their integrity. I too grew up in this atmosphere—at any rate, so far as school is concerned.

On August 11, 1919, the new Constitution of the Weimar Republic was made public. It was a significant work in its own right, but it was not exactly what was needed for a nation in Germany's position. The Germans, in the midst of defeat, were plunged into a parliamentary democracy for which their political abilities had not been sufficiently matured. Yet the Weimar Republic did not founder because of its Constitution, but rather because individual leading groups and personalities had weaknesses for which, indeed, no provisions had been made in the Constitution. Toward the middle of the 1920s, we candidates for graduation received a copy of the Constitution, but being faithful to the history we had been taught at school, we used it as a target for air rifle practice. And on the 11th of August, which was then a holiday in honor of the Constitution of the republic, many officials who drew their salaries from the republic (especially those of the rightist middle class) took part in the celebrations without any real feeling or sympathy —or else they took no part in them at all.

A profound problem for the republic, especially evident on patriotic occasions, was the flag itself. The leaders of the Left could feel no reverence for the Black-White-and-Red of the Bismarckian Empire. The colors they revered were the Black-Red-and-Gold of 1848. But now these colors too were no longer of immediate interest. The party flag of the socialists had been the international socialist red. The colors of the Pan-German flag were also the Black-Red-and-Gold. Many hoped that Germany would unite with the disintegrated Austro-Hungarian monarchy, and in a referendum a considerable part of the Austro-Germans had voted in favor of a union, but the victors prevented it. The flag thus posed a serious problem for the republic. Those groups interested in developing foreign trade, even those politically close to the Democrats, were, for practical reasons, opposed to a change in the flag. The Reichswehr never felt happy about the new flag and neither did the conservatives.

The symbolic Black-White-and-Red thus drew together all the opponents of the new republic under that flag which, people could say, had been the banner of the German troops fighting heroically for their Fatherland.[18] Even today it is difficult to evaluate calmly and correctly the republic's decision regarding the choice of its flag.

Afterward, some details were changed, and Hitler later created his own symbol in the Swastika, which had already been carried by the Freikorps and, especially, by Captain Hermann Ehrhardt's brigade, which supported the Kapp Putsch,[19] and had primarily an antisemitic significance. When Hitler came into power, he at first favored the Black-White-and-Red, but later he introduced the Swastika everywhere, sometimes combining the two in ways invented by his evident lack of taste.

Chapter Four

The Weimar Republic

The Treaty of Versailles went into effect on January 10, 1920. Germany was faced with tremendous problems and with the arduous task of reconstruction. Most people, even most Social Democrats, regarded the want of the state and of the people with alarm. Only a few radicals forgot the nation's misery in their joy at the victory of the revolution, which was actually rather the success of a mutiny occurring at the end of a war that had become unbearable. Yet many of the people, from all segments of society, were honestly ready to serve the new government. Among these were many who had been supporters of the monarchy until November 1918 and who, even now, looked upon a constitutional monarchy as the most suitable form of government for Germany. But, under the circumstances, they considered it their duty to Germany to serve the new government so that the nation might begin a new life. New dangers were now continually threatening from outside. The French, for example, tried again and again to consolidate their position on the Rhine with the help of their army of occupation.

But one thing at least had been saved, the unity of the German Reich that had been founded by Bismarck—even if it was somewhat mutilated. Heavy burdens rested upon this Reich; what the claims of the victorious powers for reparations were to be, had still not been settled, and at the same time the value of the German currency sank almost from day to day. The inflation had become apparent even to the laymen as the prices continued to rise. Germany had lost two million of its people in the war. In a weakened condition, utterly fagged out, shaken in its faith in itself and in others, Germany now had to find its way back to a completely changed world.

The internal disturbances, which had been instigated by the Communistic Spartacists and had repeatedly flared up since the spring of 1919, had now virtually been quelled. The republic seemed secure in spite of some setbacks in 1920. The boundaries in the east had been drawn up in accordance with the agreements, which had for the most part turned out favorably for Germany. East Prussia was separated from the rest of the Reich by the Polish Corridor, and a sizable part of Upper Silesia was lost. Those are (with the inclusion of the Saar territory) what today we call the boundaries of 1937, and which are found on many maps, for example, those on German railroads. The boundaries were painful to accept, but they still enclosed a large Germany—not comparable with today's!

But now the Reich was threatened anew from within, namely from the Right—by the Kapp Putsch.[1] Militarily, it was carried out by General von Lüttwitz and by Ehrhardt's Naval Brigade, which was stationed at Döberitz, in the vicinity of Berlin. Some of the soldiers had fought in the East as Freikorps, a unit that was now to be dissolved. Politically, it was led by certain men of the Right—for the most part personally blameless—who, however, proved that the class which had at one time led Germany had lost contact with reality. One can say from a historical viewpoint that the uprising had to come—and had to fail.

On the morning of March 13, 1920, the rebellious troops moved into Berlin. We schoolboys were jubilant that day, when our janitor came into our classroom with an announcement and shouted to the teacher: "The monarchists have occupied Berlin." The republican government retreated to Stuttgart; but the major part of the Reichswehr remained loyal to the government, to which it had sworn its allegiance, as did the preponderance of the bureaucracy; furthermore, the workers went out on a general strike. After four days the affair came to an end. In the Ruhr district trouble of a different sort appeared; there the workers now attacked, under extreme leftist leadership, and a red army was formed, which was ultimately defeated by the Reichswehr. In the course of the fighting the Reichswehr had entered the zone that, according to the terms of the Treaty of Versailles, was to be kept clear of German troops. Accordingly, the French had grounds for expanding the territory they occupied, and for a time they occupied Frankfurt and Darmstadt. Thus the national rioters had indirectly played into the hands of Germany's enemies, while claiming that they wanted to relieve the government of its duties because of its weakness in dealing with the enemy.

The abortive uprising had far-reaching results. Later it was looked upon as the failure of the old conservative Right, although many of the rightists had remained aloof from it. It showed that no political group could establish itself, if its ends were solely reactionary and its basic motive only contempt for the republic and the actual condition of affairs. The failure of the Kapp Putsch prepared the way for the, at first, gradual rise of Hitler.[2]

One cannot maintain that the republic was strengthened by the failure of the uprising. Its government had not used the military to defend itself in Berlin, although Reinhardt had favored such a move. After the revolt Noske resigned his position as minister of defense, because he felt he had been betrayed by some of his leading officers. Reinhardt followed suit, and thus Hans von Seeckt, one of the most opaque figures of the Weimar period, became head of the army. Otto Gessler became Noske's successor.[3]

In general, the year 1920 brought about a weakening of the forces that had built the republic and had sustained it, and a strengthening of the opposing forces, both on the Right and on the Left. The creator of the Weimar Constitution, Hugo Preuss, said at that time: "The German people toss and turn, as if burning with a fever, now to the right, now to the left, in the belief that this makes it easier to endure . . . but the fever is in its blood." Mrs. Elly Heuss commented further: "Now the German people have rolled to the right and to the left at the same time. The result is that they are breaking apart. Not one of the victorious parties . . . wants to take over the government. After seeing how those who attempt to do so are exposed to mudslinging, it is, of course, not very enticing." [4]

Two expressions are worth noting in these passages. Preuss uses the word "fever," Elly Heuss affirms that each government is smeared with mud. These are significant descriptions of the attitude of the people toward the events that had taken place since 1918. In those years preparations were being made for what was to happen after 1933 and lead to the catastrophe that lasted till 1945.

"Fever" and "the smearing of government officials"—both were prevalent on the Right and on the Left. But the course of things from 1921 on developed in such a way that danger from the Left decreased, whereas the danger from the Right, though from an entirely different Right from any hitherto known, became greater. This does not mean that Communist forces or those close to Communism were willing to forego any opportunity to gain control of the state, but they were never strong enough to do it. They did not seriously attempt a revolution after 1924, because they were ineffective, and because this weakness was recognized by their high command (which had its seat not in Germany, but in Russia), and not because they had any respect for democracy or for the republic. Also, since the economic crisis of 1930, Communism never again grew strong enough to attack, although it regained some of its strength later. The army was always its bitter enemy, the Reichswehr, as small as it was, would always have suppressed any uprising from the Left with ease and with pleasure. The claim that after 1930 it was necessary to support Hitler in order to prevent Germany from becoming Communistic has no foundation. How weak the Communists were in the crisis of the winter of 1932–33 was revealed by their almost complete defenselessness after the burning of the Reichstag, at the end of February 1933.

At the beginning of the 1920s the Communists were either idealists who actually believed in the possibility of equality in the state and in society—among these were some literary men and some intellectuals—or they were workers, who wanted to improve their position, were less interested in an ideal state, and felt that the social revolution of 1918 had not gone far enough. The mass of the people who voted Communist belonged to this group.

For the younger readers, who know only the Communist problem of the present day, I must point out the following: In those years the reality of Communism was not known outside Russia—the one country where it was established. People could still deceive themselves. But today it is otherwise. Today everyone who wants to know, can know that the reality of Communism corresponds less to the ideals of freedom and equality than any other form of government in the whole of the European world. The Communist states are among the states in which people enjoy the least amount of freedom and have the least equality.

To this it must be added that, at the beginning, the Russian revolutionary state was considerably more idealistic than it was in later times. Read, if you will, the pedagogical novels of Makarenkow [5] and you will discern in them the life and vigor that marked the beginning. This has changed. The position of German Communism today has been determined by knowledge of these facts. From the Communist standpoint it is a calamity that if a secret ballot, which would include the "eastern zone," were to be held in Germany today, Communism would receive far fewer votes now than it did in the republican Germany of 1930—even when the fact is taken into account that quite a few of the youth in the "eastern zone" would vote Communist for the simple reason that they are given no opportunity to make comparisons.

So much for the danger to the Weimar Republic from the Left. Now to the danger from the Right, and thus to the very danger to which the republic finally succumbed. We must, however, try to forget this fact for the first few years.

"Swastika on the Steel Helmet, Emblem of Black-White-and-Red . . ." these are the first words of the marching song of the Ehrhardt Brigade. These two lines contain three symbols that concern us here. I have already spoken of the power of the colors, Black-White-and-Red. Here we have, too, the Steel Helmet—by that time never merely a helmet. The steel helmet introduced to Germany in 1916 (the Western powers, taking the lead in this as in other technical matters, had already used it) became the German Steel Helmet, worn, in modified form, by the armed forces until 1945. Well shaped and virile, it became the symbol of the warrior in the hard battle of machines—the symbol of the changed face of war in general. The fact that this symbol was later often misused, also by people who had never worn a steel helmet in battle, does not change anything of its original significance.[6]

"Swastika on the Steel Helmet, Emblem of Black-White-and-Red. . . ." Of the three, the Swastika remains. When the song was first sung the Swastika was a general sign for thoughts then customarily designated as "Germanism." Here again we dare not judge only with our present knowledge. We cannot ridicule these ideas and call them "romantic," or point out that they led to the mass execution, carried out in Germany's name, of six million people. Originally the term "pure German," the German translation of the term "national," belonged to the vocabulary of the Pan-Germans; it went with the image of a basic core of Teutonic-German nationhood. This was the interpretation that had a definite effect around 1919 and later. This too we must try to understand. The long war, and in its wake revolution and collapse, had produced many unfortunate phenomena, for example, the understandable need of many people, after four years of privation, to satisfy their hunger for enjoyment. Though again the very ones who had suffered the least privations were most conspicuous.

All this led to disgusting manifestations in Berlin and in other large cities. The German Youth Movement, as a predominantly nonpolitical group, was among others an organization that directed its efforts against this. So, naturally, did the churches, and so did all who considered themselves part of a movement for the revival of "Germanism." Much idealism and unselfishness was at work here. The trouble was that the basic ideas of these "Germanistic" idealists were vague; nobody had a clear conception of the essence of the Nordic, the Germanic, or of the essence of "race" itself. Soon, however, the negative aspect was played up exclusively: hatred of the Jews—antisemitism. It had been strong before 1914, especially in Austria, but in Germany too. German antisemitism had distinguished itself before 1914 through the sordid imagination of some of its leaders, who had transformed all that lurked in the darkness of their own souls into a Jewish characteristic. Then came, after 1918, the search for a scapegoat. This search was already the motivating power behind the "stab in the back" idea. The "others" were always to blame, either the socialists, or now, the Jews.

Prejudice against the Jews is very old. It is basically a part of the Christian world, and even to the present it inheres in the world of the Christian churches. The Jews as merchants, as moneyed people—even in the Middle Ages extensive persecution of the Jews took place. The Jewish cattle dealers in the country, the Jewish moneylender—Christianity, at least in its earlier history, rejected the system of charging interest. German antisemitism did not become virulent, dangerous, and utterly abnormal until 1918.

It was forgotten that many Jews had fought in the army and, in spite of the prejudices in the military ranks, had become officers. The first delegate of the German Reichstag who volunteered and then fell in 1914 was a lawyer from Mannheim, a Social Democrat, Ludwig Frank. His picture later hung in the Reichstag, next to that of another delegate who had fallen, the Guelph, Hans von Meding. Prussian-German national myth ignored the death of both of these delegates, because they belonged to the parties that were regarded as unpatriotic; Meding's death was ignored, because he belonged to the Guelphs [7] who had held out against the annexation of Hanover by Bismarck (1866) and had clung to the ruling dynasty; that of Frank, because he was a Social Democrat and a Jew.[8]

As a consequence of the events of 1918 many Jews streamed in from the East, and a number of them rapidly enriched themselves, taking advantage of the unsettled conditions—just as many non-Jews did. But the entire German rightist press played up the Jewish scandals, even though the Jews involved were rejected by the majority of the old German Jewish population just as they were by the rest of the German people.

But in all this something quite different was playing an important part. The war had shaken not only the old authorities' influence in the state, in society, and in education but had also shaken the faith in the ability of intelligence and reason to grasp the realities of life. It can be shown, that in many areas of cultural life antirational climate often produced a proper adjustment of the one-sided intellectual view. A way had been made for this antirationalism before 1914, but it became an actual, controlling phenomenon only as a result of the war. This rejection of reason became especially fundamental in the world of politics. One symptom of it was the acceptance and promulgation by German scholars of the concept of the "stab in the back." Antisemitism was a similar case. Here a mythical belief in the power of blood was combined with the search for a scapegoat and at the same time showed a typically German inferiority complex also at work.

There was and is antisemitism in other lands also, which becomes the more powerful the less mature the people are politically. But the big European countries, especially England, assimilated their Jewish population in such a fashion that leading statesmen have been Jews, for example, in England, Disraeli and Lord Reading. In Germany this had been impossible before 1918 for social reasons, although Bismarck had been closely associated with Jews in financial affairs and had personal connections with Jewish bankers. Among the antisemites in Germany the Jew, Walther Rathenau, who had rendered outstanding services on behalf of the German war-economy was not spoken about. Nor did they mention the leading Jewish shipowner, Albert Ballin, who as the head of HAPAG [9] had achieved much for the reputation of Germany and stood close to the Kaiser, and who finally committed suicide over the German disaster of 1918.

"Swastika on the Steel Helmet. . . ." The symbol of the race hatred of "Germanism" combined with the symbol of the warrior! We schoolboys stamped small Swastikas out of the soft emergency paper money, and I recall sitting down next to the only Jewish boy in our class and trying to explain to him that it only expressed my political views and had nothing to do with our comradeship. He laughed somewhat bitterly, for he was politically more mature than I.

What we children eagerly absorbed at that time was, unfortunately, the political world of many adults. Especially so for those younger adults who after the war (during it they had grown to maturity) could not adjust to a world of peace; they had barely learned to know that world when they were called up for military service. Then there was the continual presence of the mercenaries, who had fought in the Freikorps and who, now that the problems of the eastern border and those of internal disturbances had been solved, found nothing more to do. There were others, who had never learned anything but how to be soldiers. There were many older men, officers and noncommissioned officers, who had lost their profession when the army was reduced to 100,000 men, in compliance with the Treaty of Versailles. Many of them made the change-over with success, many others merely languished and sought to identify those whom they held responsible for their misfortune. The wartime enemies of Germany were out of reach, so the new state had to bear the brunt of it, or the "November criminals," or, simply, the Jews.

If a section of the so-called academicians made so little use of their common sense, how could one expect professional soldiers who had been thrown off their course, or any other group that had been especially harmed by the disaster, to do so—for instance, those who had been expelled by the Bolsheviks; or the Baltic Germans, who had been dispossessed by the new Baltic states; or the seamen of the merchant marine, which had almost completely been given over to the Allies; or those who returned home from the territories that had been ceded to the Allies? There was much incendiary material lying around.

During the national emergency of the summer of 1919 two events had brightened the days for patriotic circles. In front of the Berlin Armory, the museum of the Prussian army, students burned flags captured in previous wars, which were now to be turned over in accordance with the Treaty of Versailles. And, at the same time, that is, just before the signing of the peace treaty, German warships, which were supposed to be handed over, were scuttled in the Bay of Scapa Flow by their crews, who had first raised the old war flags. This had a profound effect at the time, for some of these ships were the same that had flown the red flag during the mutiny of early November 1918 and had thus touched off the revolution. The self-confidence of the German navy was somewhat bolstered by this, but the basic damage remained. The navy, for the most part, joined the Kapp uprising, and during the Hitler era its leadership, at any rate, exposed it to the influence of the dictator.

This was the one world of the Germans; it spoke of the "stab in the back," of the brave deed of Scapa Flow, and of "the day," meaning the day on which the German humiliation would be avenged.

Let us now look again at the other extreme. I must first of all say that there was a strong middle group which also exercised a certain guiding influence in the state; these were the moderate Nationalists, the Catholic Center, the Democrats, and a large part of the Social Democratic party. But the world of this middle group did not penetrate far into the sphere of feelings and emotions. It remained too much in the "routine actuality"; its representatives misconstrued the situation to the extent that they did not see that more had been set in motion than mere political forms. About this I have more to say later.

Now to look at the world of the leftists. I shall proceed from the Extreme Left, but many of the points I shall make are also valid for the Social Democrats. The leftists did not talk of the accomplishments of the German army in war, but rather of injustices and of ill-treatment—which were unavoidable in such a gigantic war machine. They talked of the "achievements of the revolution," especially of the equal voting privileges in Prussia, and of the eight-hour day, and of that which was still to be attained. Above all, it seemed to these people that the power of the old classes of society was still too great.[10]

When it came to particular questions, there was a divergency of opinion. Those who were in favor of the Majority Socialists were generally also for cooperating, in a democratic and parliamentary fashion, with the existing government. They hoped that the broader goals would thereby also be attained, and though they distrusted the rebuilding of the army, they had more or less confidence in such Social Democrats as Ebert, who now represented the state.

However, those who stood further to the Left, Independent Social Democrats and Communists, did not regard the revolution of 1918 as a final revolution but were ready for another one; they were more concerned about what had not been achieved than with what had. The fact that the government was supported or tolerated by a democratic majority did not disturb them. They hoped for a dictatorship of the proletariat. Only comparatively few of these were actually trained to think according to Leninist dialectic; the masses who followed this group simply reacted according to their feelings. We must not confuse the group that is in power in Pankow [11] today with the great number of the old Communists, and especially not with the members of the old Independent Social Democratic party.[12]

While the groups both on the extreme Right and on the extreme Left fought against each other, and while both attacked the Centrists, who were supporting the government, the state, controlled by the Centrists, was continually being endangered. The pressure from the outside did not let up, the inflation mounted, and money kept on depreciating. Agriculture was the least affected by the inflation—this was the time when people said that the large-scale farmers had bought Bechstein pianos for each of their daughters. On the whole, industry, which had full employment, was also barely affected. The most strongly affected were the middle classes in the widest sense—all people who had saved under a solvent Germany and who lived on fixed salaries or pensions. This class was affected in its ways of thinking as well as in its ways of living. Intellectually and politically confused, and almost thrown off balance by the events that had occurred since 1918, the middle classes now experienced financial disaster.

Many critics, both foreign and domestic, regard the inflation as the principal reason why wide circles of the German middle class fell victim to the exceedingly primitive propaganda of the National Socialists. This I consider a one-sided view. Their helplessness in the face of the events that had taken place since 1918 is the basic thing; the inflation merely augmented this perplexity by removing the financial foundation and destroying the world of economic ideas.

On March 13, 1920, the Kapp Putsch had taken place, and on March 31st a man was released from the army who had served as a political agent after he had emerged from the war as a corporal—Adolf Hitler. He was born in Braunau on the Inn River, on April 20, 1889 and was the son of an Austrian customs official. This customs official himself was the illegitimate son of a servant girl whose name was Schickelgruber. She later married a man named Hitler, who adopted her son as his own and gave him the name of Hitler. Two things are worth noting here: "Heil Schickelgruber" would not have had the appeal of "Heil Hitler." And this man, who afterwards demanded that every German give proof of his ancestry, could certainly never have named his own grandfather on the paternal side.

All kinds of legends have become associated with this fact, such as, for instance, that his grandfather had been a Jew, and that for this reason Hitler's hatred of the Jews was explainable; this is impossible to prove and also, for various reasons, unlikely. One thing must be said here: Hitler, who was one of the most brutal haters we know of in history, generated such a strong hatred in return, that much of what his opponents said about him is just as untrue as the statements which this master of lies himself uttered.

We know little that is definite about his youth.[13] He completely beclouded the whole issue in his book *Mein Kampf*. Up to 1914 his life had been a frustrated one; the Academy of Art in Vienna twice refused him admission.

His political impressions were formed in Vienna. At the heart of these was Pan-Germanism, which favored the ascendancy of the German element in the Austro-Hungarian empire and, above all, a crass form of antisemitism, which fitted well into his smattering of education. At the outbreak of the war in 1914 he lived in Munich, where he registered as a volunteer, and although after four years he had become only a corporal, he certainly won the Iron Cross, Second Class, and, possibly, also the Iron Cross, First Class. During the revolution he lay in a military hospital. Then he became an agent of the army and thus came into contact with a group which called itself the "German Labor Party." He did not become its seventh member, as he claimed (the group already had seventy members when he came). In keeping with Austrian and German-Bohemian reminiscences he called the organization the National Socialist German Labor party.[14]

The Hitler of that time was not yet the Hitler of the later period, but he manifested some of the characteristics that helped him rise to power. He made brilliant propaganda speeches, which sounded convincing to the more naive among his listeners; he was adept at oversimplifying and at exaggerating, as well as at distorting; and he had a good memory for political and military affairs. With the last he later bewildered generals, who did not detect the infantile nature of this ability. With his fanatical passion he was able to fascinate his hearers, though at the same time he repelled others who had cooler natures and sensed all that was worthless and contradictory in his speeches.

Characteristic of the times is the situation that led to his rise to power. Hitler began his career in Bavaria during the years 1920 to 1923. There, under the protection of Bavarian particularism and pleasure in noisy spectacle, a so-called Bavarian

national climate of opinion was formed, which became inten-
sified as a result of one mass meeting after another in the
famous beer halls. Then, between 1930 and 1933 Hitler made
his way to power through the economic crisis. He took ruthless advantage of the people's despair by making promises that
often were not consistent. But many people simply wanted
something new, and at that time many, who had been critical
of him earlier, succumbed to his demonic powers. "They let
their emotions run away with them," it was said, in spite of
the warning voice of their own reason.

I shall discuss later how Hitler was able to coerce the strong,
the positive, and the idealistic forces to become his followers.
One thing must be pointed out to the younger readers by way
of admonition: Even students often laugh today when they see
Hitler in a newsreel and they ask, "How could a man with
such a blank face, which was certainly not 'Nordic,' lash all
the Germans into furious enthusiasm over his race theory?
How could Prussians, conscious of their tradition, or South
Germans, who loved their freedom, be taken in by him?"
Things are not as simple as that, and the generation of Germans before this one was not as stupid as one might sometimes think. This problem will continually confront us in
what is to come.

In the first place, we must understand the power inherent,
after 1918, in the simple idea of combining the "Nationalistic"
and the "Socialistic." This was really an ideal of many circles,
and especially of middle-class youth. It had become obvious
that the upper classes of the old state had paid too little attention to winning the working class over to their side; and on
the other hand, it was hoped that the working class would
show stronger national feelings. Hitler himself had never
spoken merely of the alleged "stab in the back." Whenever he
had made charges against the "November criminals," he had
also made them against the old ruling classes. Link the Nationalistic and the Socialistic—this slogan can be found not merely

in the doctrine of what later became the National Socialist party; the seeds of this lay in the old opinions of Friedrich Naumann.[15]

At first, however, this Adolf Hitler, who one day was to turn the world upside down and send millions to their death, played a subordinate role. Other men were more important. After the Kapp Putsch the domestic situation never really became quiet. Political agitation from both extremes increased, especially from the Right. In 1921 Erzberger and Rathenau became its victims. It was the period of political murder. Now, in addition to the "Swastika on the Steel Helmet, Emblem of Black-White-and-Red . . ." came assassination. It should be said that up to that time assassinations had not been a part of the national tradition of Germany.

Erzberger had signed the armistice in 1918, when the army considered it right, at the last moment, not to send a general as leader of the delegation. Before that, he had been hated by the rightists for being the author of the Peace Resolution of 1917 and afterward was unpopular because of the rapid adjustment he made to the new circumstances. He was a gifted and efficient man, but he was a somewhat controversial personality even in his own Center party.

The murderers of Rathenau did not even know who he was. They never dreamed that he had performed great services for Germany, and that he had appealed for national resistance as late as October 1918, when the Right had given up hope. They—two army officers—had been ordered to commit the murder; they had been told that this man was a Jew, and that was sufficient. Shortly before, in Rapallo,[16] Rathenau had delivered Germany from international isolation by a treaty with Russia. But of what concern was that to these assassins? They were ignorant, and they obeyed the orders of their secret organization, which was concerned not with Germany but with gaining power in Germany.

In German history the year 1923 can rightly be called a year of destiny. Whoever turns to those pages today can only marvel that German unity survived that year. That it did survive was the great accomplishment of the leading men of the republic, a fact that has never been properly appreciated by the Germans. In January 1923 the French occupied the Ruhr territory, because Germany was behind by 1½ percent in its reparations payments for 1922. This was the height of the ruthless French policy: "To the victor belong the spoils," for which they were later to pay dearly. For the time being, however, it brought Germany to the edge of the abyss. The government announced a policy of "passive resistance," but a new government under Gustav Stresemann had to renounce it, because the German Mark sank lower and lower.

Bavaria, which had been following an egocentric policy of its own, now became the stage for the Hitler uprising. In Saxony and in Thuringia the Social Democrats and the Communists joined forces to form governments against the rightists, who were already dominating the scene in Bavaria—Germany was on the verge of disintegration.

It should be noted here that the most serious crisis in Germany did not come immediately after the collapse of 1918, but only five years later, when it endangered the first attempts at rebuilding. The French, from without, the radical rightists and leftists, the Bavarian particularists, the more or less mild separatists in the Rhineland—all were reviling Berlin; and many rats and would-be rats wanted to leave the ship, which now finally threatened to sink, just when slowly a beginning was being made to repair the damages that had accumulated during the war and in 1918.

You must try to realize how the value of money had depreciated. In January 1923 the dollar, which in peace time was worth 4 Marks, 20 Pfennigs, had risen to 1800 Marks, and in the fall it stood at more than 4 billion Marks. This meant that savings as well as debts were gone; it meant that foreigners who had a couple of dollars or a pound sterling could buy

German houses; it meant that no longer could the economy be thought of in the old terms.

If in 1920 we had already heard that German people choose extremes—that was even more pertinent now. Here we must keep one thing in mind: The declaration of passive resistance by the government had again tremendously strengthened the patriotic passions. I recall clearly how we pupils stood before the Social Democratic newspaper office near our school and read flaming protests and appeals to the people against the French occupation of the Ruhr.

Germany survived the year 1923. Under the pressure of the troops sent by the national government, moderate governments were formed in Saxony and in Thuringia. The Hitler Putsch in Munich on November 9th collapsed during the march to the Commanders Hall, when a detachment of police opened fire. Ludendorff, who had participated in the march, went bravely through the police ranks. Hitler fell, or threw himself to the ground and afterwards fled. Already on the preceding night, when things looked otherwise than he had expected, he nearly lost his nerve.

During those days the German currency was stabilized—a significant feat performed by Karl Helfferich, Hans Luther, and Hjalmar Schacht. Germany was suddenly poor, but at least its money would be worth something again if the stability could be maintained—and it was. During these decisive weeks the chancellor was Gustav Stresemann, the old National Liberal, who had pursued a strong Pan-German policy during the war, but who now adapted himself to the facts of the situation and achieved a great deal. He was ousted [as chancellor] by the Social Democrats in November but remained German foreign minister until his death in October 1929. In that capacity he won back a place for Germany among the great powers of the world through the Treaty of Locarno,[17] against constant opposition from the Right. He wore himself out in the service of the republic; he was only fifty-one years old when he died.[18]

Locarno, 1925! Especially to the public cognizance this pe-

riod meant a certain consolidation of the republic. But Friedrich Ebert had died in February 1925; he too was only fifty-
four years old—another man who had exhausted himself in
the service of the new state. The high office he held, and the
conscientious way in which he ran it did not prevent both
radical sides from constantly attacking him; the leftist socialists regarded Ebert as one who had been disloyal to the common
man, and they had been attacking him since the end of 1918.
Just as malicious were the attacks from the Right. The last
months of Ebert's life were embittered by a trial, during which
it was claimed that he had committed treason in 1918, when
he interceded with the leaders of the munitions strike in
order to bring it to an end. One court decision only partially
exonerated him, but it was one of those decisions that occasionally were made during the Weimar period, and which
took into account the political opinion of the majority of the
jurists rather than the historic judicial truth. There were
quite a few such decisions made, but here too only extreme
cases attracted attention. Thus the leftists could speak with
some appropriateness about "class justice," while, on the other
hand, the rightists condemned certain trials, which were actually political trials of the Weimar period, as being aimed only
against the Right.

At any rate, seen from without, and in an economic sense,
the Weimar Republic in 1925 appeared to have overcome the
crisis of its birth. It had survived the year 1923 and had stabilized the Mark—these were huge successes. And in the winter of 1923–24 it had been possible to induce American experts
to intercede in the question of German reparations payments
and thereby to prevent a one-sided exploitation by France.
The separatism that had been evident in the Rhineland had
also been rejected, both in the political and in the economic
form. From a historical point of view this separatism can be
explained by the special position the Rhineland had in relation to Prussia.[19]

One would have thought that the political system, which

had surmounted the dangers of 1923, and which had made possible the Locarno Treaty of 1925, was now "out of the woods," but this was not the case.

It was actually in a weaker condition than its leaders believed. Above all, the tremendous agitation from the Right against the system and against the leading politicians continued in every possible form. In newspapers read by rightist citizens, for example, there was a regular column written by a journalist named Stein, who called himself "Rumpelstilzchen." He wrote articles on life and society in Berlin that were a combination of common society gossip and, at times injurious, political agitation. Men who had worked for the empire since 1918 and who had rescued it from the crisis of 1923 were made to look insidiously bad, and wide circles of the usually solid German middle class took pleasure in this type of writing. What had been achieved for Germany, how far the wagon had been dragged out of the mud, was not noticed; what had not been attained and the human weakness of prominent men were brought to the fore. This was a symptom of the times. The new phrase of insult was "fulfillment politicians," that is, men who wanted to fulfill all the demands made by the victors in the war. Now, what German policy actually aimed at by yielding to the demands of the old enemy was to avoid giving them any opportunity to destroy Germany completely by encroachments like the occupation of the Ruhr. Since the final amount of reparations still had not been fixed, there was some danger inherent in the economic recovery of Germany: The victors could now point to the fact that Germany was able to pay. But such considerations of foreign policy did not stop the agitators on the domestic scene.

One symptom of the situation can be seen in the election of Ebert's successor to the presidency of the Reich. In keeping with a provision of the Weimar Constitution, which can be traced primarily to the influence of Max Weber, the president was to be elected by the people. On the first ballot seven candidates had been nominated, but none had received the absolute majority, which at that time was still necessary. On the second ballot three candidates were still in the running: a Communist; former Chancellor Wilhelm Marx for the Center; and for the Right, the German field marshal of World War I, Paul von Hindenburg. Hindenburg won with a plurality of nearly a million votes over Marx. What contributed to this victory was that the Communists retained their own candidate, and that the Bavarian Catholic party backed Hindenburg. But what was demonstrated particularly here was the strength of those forces who followed the mere sound of a military name.

Even today there is no clear picture of Hindenburg's basic personality. It is apparent, however, that large segments of the German populace looked upon him as the fatherly, kind, dependable general, the Prussian who lacked the hardness of the Prussians, "the prototype of German fidelity." Some of those who backed him already knew in 1923 that he had clearly shrunk from responsibility at the time of the Kaiser's departure for Holland. Others knew that he had done a similar thing in the months that followed. His part in the successes of the so-called pair of field commanders—Hindenburg-Ludendorff in 1914—was always disputed by the latter with ever-increasing passion and with less and less tact. Many visitors to the supreme headquarters of the war said that Ludendorff was clearly the leading spirit. Hindenburg's inability to understand anything about politics was shared by the majority of his comrades in arms, and yet, with all his weaknesses, which included also a pronounced vanity, the middle class saw in him a "father image," as one would say in the psychological terms of today.

This clearly proves that the final word is not that of all this negative criticism. Hindenburg fulfilled the duties of his office loyally, at least up to the time of his reelection in 1932. His first election seemed actually to make the republic more popular with the moderate rightists; and who can hold it against him that he was not successful in warding off Hitler, since so many others, real politicians, failed at that time? In addition, he was eighty-five years old in 1932, when the last crisis loomed. Let us recall how politicians like Franz von Papen and the Prelate Ludwig Kaas of the Center party acted toward Hitler; then the charges against Hindenburg must be practically dismissed. The treatment of him in the discussion since 1945 has not always been just, even if it be granted that toward the end, influenced by his son, he committed himself to ominous forces.[20]

The crisis of 1923 was past, Hindenburg had been elected, and in foreign affairs, by Locarno, a guarantee had been secured for the new, though smaller, Germany. Did it not seem as if the republic were stable? Had it not stood the test? [21]

Nearly all opponents of the policy of that time were opposed to the form of government. But here we can practically disregard the Left. For what was sought by the inner core of the Communist movement—namely a dictatorship of the Communist minority—had no prospect of success, though it was being disguised by propaganda that used democratic and socialistic terms. (These groups have always played practical jokes with the word "democratic," and have, unfortunately, been taken too seriously by some people, especially by unworldly intellectuals. Today, the autocracy on German territory, a state, which is ruled by a small group of party bosses helped by a foreign army, calls itself the "German Democratic Republic," although there can be no talk of its being a democracy.)

There is more to be said about the opponents to the form of the government on the other side, the Right, and more about the critics in the Center itself. By no means all who were considered to belong to the Center were satisfied with the existing form of government. Many followers of the monarchy were among them, who, though conscious of their traditions, placed this devotion in the background. A restoration of the monarchy was no longer possible because of the Kaiser's conduct and the character of his son, the Crown Prince, who was more cosmopolitan than his father, but who by no means possessed the personal authority required to recover what had been lost. In South Germany there was still strong support for the independence of the states. It existed in Bavaria, where this support was also utilized in a manner detrimental to the Reich; in Württemberg, which had chosen probably the most efficient of the princes as its king before 1918; and in Baden, where the devotion to the grand dukedom was cultivated even in far-leftist circles. But none of these dynasties in the individual states would have had any chance of influencing all of Germany.

Centrists also had doubts about the usefulness of the democratic parliamentary system, which had been so quickly introduced under the pressures existing at the time of the disaster of 1918. Voting according to proportional representation was in effect. This meant that all the votes cast for the individual parties were added together, and the seats in the Reichstag distributed accordingly. By the old system, the majority vote, each voting-district had chosen a representative, and whenever necessary, a run-off ballot had been cast. The question was raised early, whether a parliamentary state based upon a voting system of proportional representation was capable of surviving. In spite of what many people appear to believe today, this problem was not considered for the first time after the downfall of the Weimar Republic.

Let us turn again to Max Weber, whose passionate utterances regarding the problems of war I have mentioned. Weber too was deeply affected by the catastrophe of 1918 and, in January 1919, he stated that as far as utter misery was concerned, the past two months had exceeded anything known to German history.[22] He had in mind the self-condemnation of the German "intellectuals," who spoke about the question of German war guilt. He himself had always wished for an understanding with England that would have made the war impossible, but he could not stomach the idea that Germany alone was to be blamed for the war. Someone wrote to Weber at that time, "What we need now is simply an educator who will teach all the people to ponder these things in such a way that something will come of it." [23] This is the formula for our destiny: "To teach the people to ponder things so that something will come of it." But this need was not filled—of course it must be taken into account that the writer of the letter, who naturally considered Weber to be this educator, overestimated the power of a single individual. Weber was already skeptical: "A new order of things, which is the product of this terrible defeat and disgrace, will hardly take root." [24] He does not defend the new, "But despicable," he said, "unjust, and hardhearted are the cheap condemnations made at the expense of the new by supporters of the collapsed gambling party." [25] He could not anticipate it, and he did not live to see the day when these cheap judgments would help to pave the way for Hitler. From the last years of his life, after he had heard the talk of an uprising from the Right, comes this remark: "For the restoration of Germany to its former glory I would gladly make a pact with any power on earth, and even with the devil himself, but never with the forces of stupidity. As long as insane persons from the Right and Left have their way in politics, I shall remain aloof from it." [26] Rightists in their stupidity despised this man, who passionately loved his country, and insultingly called him a "Democrat." In June 1920 Max Weber died, too early for scholarship and too early for Germany.

I cannot discuss in detail the argument among the ranks of the Centrists over what form of government the state should have. But already at the beginning of the 1920s, the alert spirits saw that behind that question lay another—what the ties were that bound the people to the republic. Naturally, here foreign affairs could not be separated from domestic affairs.

Thus the historian, Friedrich Meinecke, who in 1918 had become a republican for rational reasons (as he said), now ranged himself against the Right, because he knew the past and the Right continually referred to the example set by the Prussian revolt of 1813. The "Germanists" of the present day, he said, "are able only to perceive how the great leaders of 1813 cleared their throats and spat, but they have no notion of their inward pathos." [27] In a lecture in Berlin in 1925, which I myself heard as a nineteen-year-old student, he said: "It is actually the resentment of a class which has been overthrown that makes the political atmosphere in Germany today so thick and heavy." [28] By references to Machiavelli he sought to make it clear to his student audience that it is proper in politics to look upon the lesser evil as a good thing and to stand up for it. He did not consider the parliamentary system as the ultimate solution for Germany, but he looked upon it as a transitional form. He saw the crisis of German parliamentarism and wished for a more stable government than its form at that time made possible. He also tried to be just to what he called youth's "need for heroism." [29]

That was in January 1925. In May I witnessed the entry of Hindenburg into Berlin as the new president of the Reich, and from a distance I watched him being sworn in at the Reichstag. The flags fluttered on the lances of the Reichswehr cavalry. We saw such war leaders as Alfred von Tirpitz, the representative of the German nationals, in a black coat and top hat, and Ludendorff, the "pure German" delegate, in an emphatically nonfestive, coarse jacket.

In the fall Stresemann and Luther achieved the signing of the Locarno Pact, and when Stresemann died several years later the aging Hindenburg followed his casket through the streets of Berlin. Everything seemed harmonious, everything seemed to be consolidated. German economy had practically overcome the crisis since the stabilization of the currency. When sometime later I made a trip around the world in connection with some private affairs in South America, the boys in Asiatic harbors were diving for German silver Mark pieces just as eagerly as for English shillings, which, until a short while before had been considered in Germany the very embodiment of stable wealth.

What was the political behavior of the Right during those years? Self-contradictory and inconsistent. The German Nationalists, the large party of the opposition supported by the conservative middle class, consisted, as was soon to become evident, of most heterogeneous elements. The party had enjoyed considerable success in the elections of 1924 and, according to parliamentary procedure, could hardly avoid the responsibility resulting from cooperation in government. But they did not have the courage, in foreign affairs, to "stick to their colors." When a decision on the Dawes Plan [30] was up for a vote in 1924, they furnished so many Yes votes (although they had previously fought aggressively against this settlement of the reparations, which was somewhat more moderate than the earlier plan, but still harsh), that its passage was assured. At the same time the party functionaries across the country were agitating against the so-called fulfillment politicians.

On the whole, disunity was a characteristic of this party, to which so many German academic men and their wives, Protestant pastors, and other essentially respectable people gave their votes. Many of their followers, who personally would never say anything unjust about anyone, lost these inhibitions when it came to the new state and its leaders. I remember what a shock it was for me when, at the university, groups of this political persuasion spoke about a "red brother," meaning a colleague who was known to be sympathetic to socialism (which was nearly everything that was to the left of this party) and about a "black brother," meaning a member of the Catholic Center. The rightist middle-class press published highly respected newspapers, which, however, were one-sided on this point; it published others, which would have been called the yellow press by the German Nationalist circles, if these had not represented their own thinking.

The revolution and the introduction of a parliamentary form of government had changed the political style and had made it cruder. This was evident, as rightist circles claimed, not only in socialist or leftist middle-class papers—such as the big Berlin papers, which were sympathetic to the Democratic party. Two of these were in Jewish hands and were capably edited journals. In rightist circles, people spoke of the Jewish yellow press in Berlin, but anyone who at that time read rightist newspapers in Berlin with a critical eye would have to admit that many of them had more of the yellow character than those democratic organs. But these were politically further to the Left, and that sufficed to stop people from reading them, though they condemned them all the more energetically. Here, and in similar spheres of the so-called national bourgeoisie, a deterioration in political style prevailed, which left the door wide open for an attack from such people as Josef Goebbels. One must understand that these groups felt that the revolution had caught them unawares. They did not (at least not openly) look among their own ranks to search out where the blame lay, because their own ranks were being so viciously attacked by the leftists. Instead, they fought back with weapons which several years before they would never have touched. The methods they used to defend themselves were bound to destroy their very existence, and actually did destroy it. Intending to take revenge on the "November criminals," they actually prepared their own suicide.

Thus, the attitude of the middle-class rightists made the future of Hitler, who failed in 1923, appear bright with prospect. In May 1924 the "Germanists," to whom the National Socialists later were joined, received 32 seats in the Reichstag.

The shameless and ruthless attack upon the existing order, which was important only to some of the German Nationalists, was a general practice among the "Germanists." At first only smaller groups took part in it—uprooted and disappointed socialists, but also many of the petty bourgeoisie, and quite a number of academic people, whose education had not equipped them to grasp the emptiness of this agitation.

Meanwhile the German Nationalists repeatedly became the party of government; in Hindenburg they had a president whom they could trust. He had made the republic also respectable enough for them. But even when they were in control of the government, they tolerated the discord created by their own followers throughout the country, in fact, they had to tolerate it. Some of their ministers were among the most competent ministers of the Weimar Republic. When the Pact of Locarno was being prepared, the German Nationalists favored it in the conviction that something important for Germany was being achieved. Afterward, difficulties appeared over the question of the evacuation of the Occupied Territories, that is, those territories that still were occupied. The French did not want to leave before 1930. The formal revocation of the signature approving the war-guilt clause of the Versailles Treaty was relinquished by the Germans; thereupon the German Nationalists withdrew from the government and abused Luther and, more so, Stresemann upon their return from Locarno. One thing is certain, no one else could have obtained more for Germany, and when Stresemann's letters were made public after 1930, it was evident that he had remained a passionate patriot to the very end. But the German Nationalists now had no more time for retraction; by then Hitler had attained power, and he quickly put an end to their party, whose radical Right, at any rate, had helped him to power. (Not until after 1945, when Stresemann's papers were made available, did it become completely clear how much injustice had been done to him, especially when he had been blamed for renouncing his former feelings and for not doing enough for his country.) But it was characteristic of the pseudo-nationalistic agitation of the time, that many of their otherwise very respectable leaders took no notice of these revisions. They used their own method for the moral "stab in the back." [31]

What is most instructive about the development of the domestic affairs in those years is that government crises often were a consequence of such crises in national feelings, but they were seldom a result of any specific, concrete arguments. The German Nationalists were always either the party in power, or, due to their strength, qualified to form a coalition government; but they never dared to recognize the actualities of foreign policy, because otherwise they would have lost part of their basic propaganda appeal.

On the Left things were different. To be sure, some of the so-called Majority Socialists were not quite content with the "achievements" of the revolution, or believed them to be threatened anew. The eight-hour day had been one of the achievements; industry strove to annul it at the time when full employment prevailed and when higher reparations payments were being demanded. But as far as their attitude toward the state's policies was concerned, the Social Democrats were, on the whole, satisfied; they saw that their party was still important.

People gave too little thought to "awareness of very recent history"; they failed to notice what meaning the questions connected with 1918 had for the opponents of the state on the Right. Nearly the same can be said of the middle-class parties of the Center, which supported the government, and of the government itself. These underestimated the danger that lay in the misrepresentation of recent history by the Right. "Swastika on the Steel Helmet, Emblem of Black-White-and-

Red. . . ." Everything was less noisy and excited than it had been years before, but under cover there was considerable activity.

The radical Left (the Communists) continued to hope for an overthrow. It came more and more under the direct control of Moscow but was not strengthened thereby, because, ever since Rapallo, official Moscow maintained strictly correct relations with Berlin. At the same time, in secret, close contact existed between the German and the Russian armies. German officers, especially aviators, were being trained in Russia in the use of weapons that had been prohibited in Germany under the Treaty of Versailles. Thus a close tie came into existence between the army of the Bolshevik state and those circles in Germany that were, and had to be, Communism's main enemy in the country. Until 1930, the percentage of Communist seats in the Reichstag never reached more than 13 percent, and even in the crisis of 1932 it went no higher than 18 percent. I have already pointed out that such a minority could win only by force, and that, because they could not fight against the army and the police, such a victory was impossible. Furthermore, the enmity between the Communists and the Social Democrats in the late twenties was so fierce that a teaming-up of the two so-called workers' parties of the Left was out of the question.

In the meantime Germany had become a member of the League of Nations. In 1929 an adjustment of German reparations had been adopted, and the evacuation of the remaining occupied zones was set for 1930, five years earlier than decreed in the Versailles agreement. Furthermore, foreign capital had begun to flow into Germany, and by 1928 the German economy appeared to be permanently on the upgrade. In 1929 the French statesman, Aristide Briand, and the German representative, Stresemann, found themselves working together at the League of Nations, in Geneva, for a "united Europe" in which Germany was to play the role of a great power and thus make its special contribution. Only ten years had passed since Versailles.

Only ten years. . . . The passions aroused in November 1918 and again in 1919 over the peace treaty were not dead, but in 1928 they seldom manifested themselves in everyday life. By 1930 things were different. I was overseas from May 1929 until May 1930, and when I returned to Germany the political climate had changed—the old passions were again in control of the field. How had this happened?

Some of the physical causes were quite apparent. Agriculture had, at least since 1927, taken no real part in the economic upswing, and the rest of the economy moved toward a crisis when, in 1929, the American depression became evident and began to have far-reaching effects. Because of these circumstances, but primarily for other reasons, the Reichstag became incapacitated in the winter of 1929–30 and could no longer form a majority government of Centrists.[32] This came above all from the fear among the Social Democrats of the radical leftist propaganda, and from the fear among the bourgeois rightists of the radical rightist propaganda—this, especially in the face of rising unemployment. Actually, there were only fifty Communists and twelve National Socialists among five hundred delegates, but again an undercurrent in favor of the extremes proved to be decisive. Ultimately it was a question of the final settlement of the reparations, and by this time widespread unemployment existed, since, due to the economic crisis, German exports had been sharply curtailed.

Heinrich Brüning, one of the most honest and most idealistic statesmen of the Weimar Republic, was the first chancellor who was not supported by a relatively clear majority. Especially the National Socialists fought him bitterly, accusing him, among other things, of Catholic sectarianism. This, by the way, was a totally unfounded accusation. With the exception of Göring, the most clamorous leaders of National Socialism came from the Catholic world, but they were renegades, and it is a well-known fact that the hatred of renegades is the worst kind of hatred. This can be said of Hitler and of Goebbels, who at his graduation from Heidelberg still strongly emphasized his Catholic stand, and also of Himmler. They all were deeply unjust to Brüning, an ardent and impartial patriot, who, at the most, had made one mistake, namely, that he overestimated the power of the moderate Protestant conservatives.

But of greatest importance was that Brüning, who had some inclination to the Right, received no support from the German Nationalists, because they were not willing to relinquish anything to the National Socialists. The leadership of the German Nationalists was now assumed by Alfred Hugenberg,[33] probably the most sinister figure of the German middle class in those years. He controlled the press and the movies, but he was not able to handle the National Socialists. He believed he could defeat them with their own methods. The arrogance of the old German class system was still to be seen in this belief that Hitler could be used against the Weimar Republic and then dropped. Hugenberg believed this, so did Franz von Papen, who next to Hugenberg was the most uncanny of the figures of the transition period, but who was hardly so important as Hugenberg; so did the financial wizard, Schacht. I recall a Stuttgart mass meeting in 1932 at which Hugenberg spoke. He was wearing an old-fashioned frock-coat, and what he said was: "We also are ready to fight. If necessary, even in shirt-sleeves." With this bourgeois image he showed how completely helpless he was against the new methods of the National Socialists—street-terrorism. These people were blinded by their hatred of the Weimar Republic, and did not realize that they were holding the stirrups for Hitler. Hugenberg became a member of Hitler's first Cabinet, but the latter kept none of his promises, and within a short time Hugenberg lost his power and was eliminated.

Now the old rage flared up again, about war itself and the

war's end in 1918. The leading politicians of the republic had not taken the smoldering passions seriously, and had also failed to evaluate correctly the need of youth to be addressed on its own level.

Meinecke, in his speech of 1925, had spoken of youth's need for the heroic that gave spirit to the nationalistic bent. Count Kessler, whose diaries appeared in the fall of 1961, and who apparently had leftist leanings, described as the basic characteristics of German youth the inclination to metaphysics and to some kind of belief; the urge to drill, to be commanded, and to command. He records the opinion of Fritz von Unruh, that the republic had failed to recognize the important part youth and heroism play in politics.[34] Both Kessler and Unruh [35] certainly were right about the youth of the period between the wars. Certainly the youth of that time had this "need for heroism," and the rightist youth tried to satisfy it by joining national defense leagues and, especially, the SA.[36]

Chapter Five

World War I in Literary Retrospect

Today we cannot properly assess the impact of World War I on the Europe of 1914, for today we are only too accustomed to wars and outbreaks of violence. In the Germany of 1918, that impact was at first not merely political. A nation and a people had been engaged in war for four years and now had to make a painful readjustment to times of peace. I have already pointed out that this was difficult for many. Naturally people could not forget those years and their comrades in arms who had perished—after all, two million out of a population of sixty-five million had died. Many old soldiers kept the memory of those difficult years and of their comrades alive by joining regimental organizations, by going to navy league meetings, and by keeping in contact with war associations in general. In most towns monuments to the dead were erected, and the units of the Reichswehr continued to cultivate the traditions of the imperial army. All this could be kept politically neutral, and in the beginning it was simply an expression of natural feelings. But, by embracing the old flag, Black-White-and-Red, in defiance of the existing state with its flag, Black-Red-and-Gold, the situation was politically exploited—in some instances more and in others less.

But now let us turn to the literature.[1] Here a countercurrent prevailed. With one exception, the best portraitures of the experience of war resulted from a critical or even pacifist attitude toward the war. Around 1939 this attitude seemed to predominate, for the most significant literary interpretations of the war only came in large numbers about ten years after it was over. Most of what appeared earlier had no widespread consequences; particularly not the histories of regiments and divisions with depictions of the war that were meant to keep alive or reawaken the martial spirit of the people. At the other extreme the literature of pacifism intended to spread detestation of war by describing its horrors.

Only one writer, Ernst Jünger—he lives and writes to this day—tried at an early stage to use a lasting form that would enable him to reproduce the experience of war without apparent bias, yet with complete representation of the feelings of soldiers. Jünger, who until 1923 was an officer in the Reichswehr, had published as early as 1920 a kind of war diary, *In Stahlgewittern* [In Storm of Steel]; and again and again until 1928 he tackled the war in which he had carried, at the front, the highest decoration, the Order of Merit. I consider *Das Wäldchen 125* [Woodland 125], 1925, describing trench warfare in a series of scenes, his most inclusive book in this field. Jünger is that type of man who experiences things with a strong, crystal-clear and at the same time completely cold awareness.

Shortly before 1933 he published a sociological interpretation of that time, *Der Arbeiter* [The Laborer]. The National Socialists relied upon him for a time, at least the intellectuals among them, who were soon to be pushed aside. Later, during the Third Reich, he wrote a symbolic book against the dictatorship of small men, not because of his disdain for dictatorship in general but out of contempt for this dictatorship in particular. His writings published since 1945 do not belong here.

Jünger is practically the only important writer, who, within the first eight years after 1918, expressed a consistently positive attitude toward the subject of war. But the number of his readers remained small. He had no traceable influence on the literary flood of 1928 that brought the war into prominence again, nor did he contribute anything to it himself.

The best known book from this flood of war novels written around 1928 is the work of a man who gave himself the literary name Erich Maria Remarque.[2] He too is still alive, but he emigrated in 1932, first to France (he wrote the very instructive novel about emigrés, *Arc de Triomphe*), then to America, and today he again lives in Europe. Remarque's *Im Western nichts Neues [All Quiet on the Western Front]* became an international success—the only German book about the war to do so. "All quiet on the western front" was the style used in war reports to state that no great battles had been fought (the day before), and that the daily routines of war had gone on as usual. "This book is to be neither an accusation nor a confession. . . . It will try simply to tell of a generation of men who, even though they may have escaped its shells, were destroyed by the war." (Prefatory Note.) Yet it is both an accusation and a confession. It accuses war and its advocates, and is the confession of a young man who inwardly had not been able to cope with the war, and who by means of this book freed himself from it. The manuscript was at first rejected by the Fischer press, but Ullstein published it in 1928.

This is the beginning: "We are at rest five miles behind the front. Yesterday we were relieved, and now our bellies are full of beef and haricot beans. We are satisfied and at peace." Animal contentment! This is the ending: "He fell in October, 1918, on a day that was so quiet and still on the whole front, that the army report confined itself to the single sentence: All quiet on the Western Front. . . . His face had an expression of calm, as though almost glad the end had come." [Translated into English by A. W. Wheen, 1930.]

In between is the action, that is, the suffering. The central theme is not the external war against the enemy—it does occur of course—but the battle against the enemy within, against those commanders of the war who confront the young recruits. For example, the noncommissioned officer who hounds the young soldiers at home and puts them through the grind. They take their vengeance on him when he himself finally comes to the front. The name of the man who has become the symbol for hundreds of thousands is Himmelstoss. Then there is another adversary: the schoolmaster who with his patriotic phrases had pressured the pupils to volunteer, but who himself is drafted at a very late date. Now his former pupil can get even with him—he snarls at the schoolmaster, who has now been transformed into a militiaman, with the same words that the teacher had once used to reprimand his pupils. In the end the pupil says to the exhausted teacher in the characteristic tones of a schoolmaster: "Homeguardsman Kantorek, we have the good fortune to live in a great time, when we must all make a tremendous effort to overcome all that is bitter." Brutal scorn! Later the instructor and the school janitor are ordered to pull a small wagon to fetch bread.

All Quiet on the Western Front is the book about the oppressed man who takes vengeance, and this explains its unusual worldwide success. The underdog! The book is not highminded; it often crosses the line of (what was then considered) good taste. But we must be aware of one thing: World War I was more destructive of the old order than all the radically revolutionary or socialistic ideas that came before. It not only shook the position of the white race in the world, it also led, among the white peoples themselves, to a questioning of the authorities, because these authorities had been compelled to demand too much of their followers. State and Fatherland, order and command, everything began to be questioned, and not only in the countries where the war ended in revolution, as, first of all and most significantly in Russia, Austria, and

Germany, but also in the other countries. *All Quiet on the Western Front* is an outcry, but it is the outcry of a man who no longer had either the ability or the desire to understand soldiery and the ideas associated with it.

Of more importance is a book that appeared at about the same time, but which requires much more of the reader, is more specifically German, and, above all is more definitely soldierly. It first appeared as a serial in the *Frankfurter Zeitung*, then in book form. This is Ludwig Renn's *Krieg* [War].

Ludwig Renn is also still alive, the name is a pseudonym, his real name is Arnold Friedrich Vieth von Golssenau. Renn was an officer, of noble Saxon stock, became a Communist around 1930, took part, as an officer, in the Spanish Civil War, and today lives in the Eastern Zone. Together with Arnold Zweig [3] (*Streit um den Sergeanten Grischa* [*The Case of Sergeant Grischa*], which marks the beginning of the new "Gestaltungsliteratur"), Renn, who professes loyalty to the Communist regime, is the most significant German writer of the older generation.

This does not stop me from declaring that he wrote the most important and original book about the war, both in its content and in its form; and it does not stop me from regretting that this book, even though not an iota of the Communist spirit is to be detected in it, is no longer reprinted in the Federal Republic.

Now to *Krieg*. Renn describes himself (the I-hero) not as an officer but as a soldier who is gradually promoted and who experiences the war from that angle. "I had become a corporal on the day when the mobilization began." The experiences of this Renn are shown throughout the war and include the march back and the transportation of the troops after the armistice. "Where we were going we didn't know, except that we would not be going home immediately."

The objective style of the book is achieved by transferring the viewpoint of an officer, really the author who went through the experiences, to that of a noncommissioned officer. The book belongs to the most important works of the post-expressionistic period, to the so-called new objectivity. Here one finds a style that reproduces impressions and the conscious reactions to them with uncanny fidelity. Many have learned from Renn without admitting it.

This book must not be discussed primarily as a work of art, but rather as an illustration of the world of the German soldier between 1914 and 1918. Here too we find the rejection of the "tough" superiors and of all patriotic phrases; and yet, about the collapse we read: "But I was sad. The damned Fatherland was dear to me after all." This book has brilliant character descriptions. Each person is an individual and at the same time represents a type. All are forced into one mold by the duties of the war and by its uncanny power—failures and cowards, slackers and informers, but also many who do perform their duty, outstanding soldiers some of them. Of these, Renn loves best the one-year volunteers [4] and the volunteers coming from the ranks of high school and university students. This book has two heroes, if, indeed, it has any at all. Professedly, Renn himself, a man who whole-heartedly accepts his fear and at times succumbs to it, yet he is a man who, on the whole, becomes a regularized squad leader; and a one-year volunteer, Lamm, who belongs to the group just mentioned. At first Lamm is incompetent and frail, but he proves himself in battle and becomes an excellent company leader. Renn, as writer, portrays some extremely likeable German officers of World War I, and, of course, also the opposite kind. Both are, no doubt, types he had come to know. (His later political inclinations are not yet felt here.) With equal vividness he portrays the noncommissioned officers and the enlisted men. A pen is here at work whose power of expression is far superior to Remarque's. Taken as a whole, the book describes a cross-section of German soldiers and their behavior in war without the intellectual vagueness of our exaggerated modern symbolism, and nevertheless leads to something universal in every figure and every scene. And all this is done by the most economic means—not a word too many, not a word wrong. Here we find the wellspring of behavior as it really was.

Basically, Renn was not favorably inclined toward the war, but he was not as completely opposed to the war as Remarque was. War is presented as a rigorous experience that shapes the lives of those who survive it.

Protests against fictionalized accounts of the war came from various quarters and were especially directed against Remarque; diaries and memoirs were brought forward to counteract them. From the wealth of literature that was a product of this war over the war, I have chosen only one book because, in contrast to Remarque's as well as Renn's works, it came from the political Right, and in spite of that gives an exceptionally authentic account. It was published by the Lehmann press in Munich (a house noted for its medical publications, but also known as representing a radical rightist point of view) and was written by the publisher himself, Friedrich Lehmann. The book's title is, *Wir von der Infanterie, Tagebuchblätter eines Bayrischen Infanteristen* [We of the Infantry: Pages from the Diary of a Bavarian Infantryman], 1929. "It has almost become a habit today to present books about World War I in fictionalized form. That is very convenient, for then one can embellish and enlarge one's own, sometimes meagre, experiences at will, and can conveniently include experiences gained subsequently and put them in anyone's mouth; after all, readers of a novel have no right to demand the truth." Apparently only diaries and sketches are reproduced in it to show how "unprovoked and normal German youth found the war. After reading those unmanly books by youthful old men [this is aimed at Remarque] it seemed to be my duty." It is an important book, and though it too is not entirely without political prejudices, it displaces many other books written from a similar viewpoint because it is neat and compact and without illusions about the "stab in the back." As one of the concluding quotations we find, "Things cannot go on this way."

Many other books from the literary flood around 1928 could be mentioned, but no purpose would be served by merely giving their names. Yet, in order not to limit the picture to literature that poses problems, I should like to add one more, a book that appeared in 1935 and was written by a well-known art historian, Karl Borromäus Gröber—*Mit zwei Zentnern durch den Weltkrieg. Erinnerungen eines Optimisten* [With Two Hundredweights through the World War: Recollections of an Optimist]. Gröber had also experienced heavy fighting, but he was a mature man. He writes ingenious descriptions of the battles in a succession of pointed observations. Indeed I know of no better book written by a German scholar concerning his war experiences—with or without two hundredweights to throw about.

This is only a comment intended to correct to some extent misconceptions of the literature of World War I on the part of those interested in the history of ideas. In this connection another book must not be overlooked. Even if war is not its only theme, it does proceed from the experiences of war and would not have been written without them. It was published before the literary flood of 1928. In 1926 the two large volumes of a novel—*Volk ohne Raum* [A People Without Living Space]—by Hans Grimm appeared. Grimm had been a merchant in Southwest Africa and had published his *Südafrikanische Novellen* [*South African Short Stories*] before World War I.

Volk ohne Raum—a signal! Here he means the struggle for colonies overseas. War here is a colonial war, that is, not war in Europe, in which millions of soldiers participate, but rather war far from home, in which a few thousand Germans take part. But this experience of war is only the turning point of an often long-winded story about German fortunes during the closing decades of the nineteenth century and is part of an argument with England that runs through the whole book. Grimm's mixture of love and hate is typical of the feeling of many Germans toward the British—feelings that represent the most curious aspect of the attitude of the Germans toward other nations. In his dedication Grimm says: "This narrative about Germans, I believe, is a political story and by these means shows the workings of our destiny; this is certainly not what is taught in schools and by parties, because they are neither willing nor able to do so." The book closes with a vague description of a type of National Socialism.

Today, Hans Grimm's novel is not considered a serious literary work by German *avant-garde* writers and critics. As a narrator, Renn is a whole generation ahead of Grimm, but Grimm has his place, too.

Several years ago Grimm died—an embittered man. He had at first supported Hitler, was misused by Goebbels to write propaganda, and as a result was ill-treated after 1945. Then he wrote pamphlets filled with hatred, which showed that his artistic ability was exhausted and that his politics had led him down a blind alley. After 1926 he did have far-reaching influence. His *Volk ohne Raum* must not be overlooked if one would understand the turn to radicalism of German youth after 1930.[5]

How did this flood of books on the war influence German history around 1930? Hardly at all. The narrative style of the most valuable works had rejected catchphrases, so that they, like the definitely pacifistic attitude of Remarque and others, were hardly understood by the generation then growing up. Youth around 1930, accustomed to the newly won prosperity, were mostly not interested in politics, they were "impartial" —as it was called at that time. When a movie was made of *All Quiet on the Western Front,* rightist groups demonstrated against it, but this occurred during and after 1930, as a consequence of newly roused passions.

Among the followers of National Socialism, which was now in ascendancy, only war literature that tended to glorify war was given encouragement, although at first some of the more moderate books were also retained. But the thorough falsification of recent German history—Hitler was its most avid prophet—did not spare this field either. In *Mein Kampf* Hitler also repeatedly refers to his own war experiences. One point has not yet been clarified: Why did this man, who apparently earned the Iron Cross, First Class as corporal, never become a noncommissioned officer, since he was certainly not unintelligent? [6]

The decisive fact about these proceedings, which, both in literature and in politics, brought the war to the surface again after it had been over for ten years and more, was that they affected young people who had never actually experienced this war. Of those who had participated in the war many were made uncomfortable by the situation. Many, unlike Remarque, did not regard themselves as having been shattered by the war and basically condemned the exploitation of the recent war for the purpose of the radicalization of domestic politics. Many of them regarded any literary interpretation of the war with distrust. Those who spoke noisily about the war at friendly get-togethers, at organization meetings, or at social gatherings, were usually not the ones who had been at the front or had especially distinguished themselves in battle. Others took it upon themselves to make sure that the military tradition was preserved among the German people—in spite of Versailles—but what they strove for was ultimately misused by Hitler and the National Socialists. The two million, however, who had died for Germany were condemned to silence. Everyone extolled them—the pacifists, in order to condemn war, the defenders of war, because they seemed to want to give the sacrifice its proper significance. What they did, however, was give it a significance that was of their own making and not the one inherent in the sacrifice.

Chapter Six

The End of the Republic

Those years after 1930 seemed almost ghost-filled. Though crucial political problems were publicly dealt with, it was over these specters of the past that a far more passionate dispute was carried on at the same time; a dispute over the interpretation of Germany's most recent history—the war and the end of the war. All this took place before the eyes of the youth who at the end of the war had been only a few years old.

The most feverish year was 1932. Hindenburg was reelected president of the Reich with the help of the votes of the Social Democrats; Hitler, running against Hindenburg, attracted not merely the votes of the National Socialists but also of most of the German Nationalists. Many of us were somewhat perplexed at that time because we kept coming across people who were otherwise quite rational, but who declared that they were voting for Hitler. Various reasons for this were given by those who were not National Socialists. Some said this would be the best way to render him harmless; others simply said that some sort of change would have to be made. Within one year the situation had indeed changed, so much so that this particular group of voters for Hitler trembled with horror.

A peculiar uncertainty had gripped the leaders of the existing government ever since the dissolution of parliament in 1930. In the elections for the Reichstag in September 1930 the

National Socialist representation had suddenly jumped to over 100 seats and Dr. Heinrich Brüning was placed in the position of having to govern without a parliament, and having to rely instead upon the so-called emergency decrees of the Weimar Constitution.[1]

In every succeeding election new splinter parties appeared (hence the necessity for the Five Percent Clause in Germany's voting law today).[2] Hindenburg, now eighty-five, allowed himself to be influenced against Brüning. Materialistic interests played a sinister part here and the so-called measure in aid of agriculture in the East was one of the factors involved. The republican tax money intended for that section had been distributed too liberally by groups who were against the republic. At the end of May 1932 Hindenburg suddenly dismissed Brüning. As his successor he named Franz von Papen, a man who until then had been virtually unknown.

From then on the direct path to Hitler was open, though this was not the intention of the government. The Papen government, aside from the chancellor himself, consisted of some outstanding professionals, but it had a primitive restoration program. Papen overthrew the Prussian government with the help of the army, and it was a shock to Social Democracy as a whole (from which it has actually not recovered to this day), that such Prussian Social Democrats as Otto Braun and Carl Severing, who had until then been considered strong, gave in without a struggle. This clearly shows that since 1919 the leadership that was needed had not existed.

Discord now reigned at all levels. The fights, which occurred in public halls and on the streets of large cities, attracted to the National Socialists some of the hoodlums who up to that time had fought on the side of the Communists. The setting was by no means always political. At times it smacked of the underworld, as is clearly shown by the unsavory history of Horst Wessel, the composer of the party song of the National Socialists, "Die Fahne hoch." [3]

On a more idealistic level were the arguments among the students who quite early had been exposed to a kind of radical National Socialism as a consequence of "Germanist" and nationalistic rightist currents, in which the passions already mentioned had played an especially important part after 1918. But as far as youth was concerned only enthusiasm and unselfish devotion were poured into the National Socialist movement—by students, by pupils, and also by young workers. The destitution in agricultural circles turned whole areas radical and pushed many young farmers and agricultural workers into the arms of National Socialism. None of these were inhibited by political experience; they thought "heroically" and like all enthusiastic young people of all times they thought for the most part "utopically," which means that they did not think of possible ways to make their dreams come true; the ideal alone sufficed. It was compared with the existing state of affairs in Germany, its many parties, its unemployment and—as was believed—its national disgrace. Little thought was given to history; the ideal was projected into the personalities of the leaders of National Socialism. Among these, however, only the personal appearance of Hermann Göring, the combat aviator of World War I, came close to such an image.

Hitler wanted to do justice to all such notions held by his heterogeneous followers. He knew how to handle youth, and in other respects he is best described as representative of the ideal of the German lower middle class. He liked to be photographed often with children, especially with blond boys and girls, though he scarcely exchanged a word with them. He pretended to be a self-sacrificing man; even as chancellor and leader of the Reich he maintained that he had no personal bank account. Since then it has been ascertained that he received tremendous sums from the sale of his book alone. To what extent Hitler later believed his own lies is difficult to say—during the war, at any rate, he became a victim of his own propaganda.

At noon on the 30th of January 1933 a special edition of the Tübingen paper came out: Hitler had become chancellor of the Reich. Some people laughed, saying that it would not last long; others rejoiced; still others remained silent, numb with horror. Never did a majority of the German people in a free election choose Hitler to direct the course of German destiny, but he was the leader of the strongest party and, according to parliamentary procedure, he had to take the reins of government. What occurred behind the scenes in those days people at that time did not know. General Kurt von Schleicher had been chancellor for a short while, since December 1932. He had been a political general, and because Hitler executed him in 1934 considerable uncertainty exists today concerning his motives; he has become a convenient scapegoat for many. Schleicher had also underestimated the danger presented by Hitler, though he had taken it more seriously than Papen. In January 1933 Hitler allied himself with important financial and industrial groups against Schleicher, and on January 30th Hindenburg reluctantly gave in—Hitler was to form a cabinet including Papen (as vice-chancellor) and Hugenberg (as minister).

They all continued to underestimate Hitler. Hugenberg was ousted within a short time, and Papen was stripped of his power. Even his opponents underestimated Hitler. Theodor Heuss wrote a book about Hitler in 1932 in which he warned against the adventurer and the hater; afterward he repeatedly said that in it Hitler had been underestimated. Like a new Pied Piper of Hamelin, this man attracted all people who wanted something different or new: the youth who believed in the greatness and integrity of Germany's future; the older people who hoped that Germany would soon wage a war to avenge Versailles; and the farmers who hoped that he would support their market by raising the prices of their produce. He also attracted the workers, because he had promised them higher wages concurrent with lower prices for food and, especially, employment for all; the industrialists, because he had promised them social peace, that is, they were to have workers who would not go on strikes. Old soldiers extolled the corporal with the Iron Cross, First Class. Nature lovers praised the man who supposedly was a vegetarian. Women voted for the man with the dark hair and the blue eyes. All who hoped that he would put an end to their peculiar miseries or who expected him to give them special help voted for him. He juggled with promises and complaints and maintained that where all others had failed he alone could and would improve everything.

He was certainly given to hysteria, but the people themselves had become hysterical after 1930, and he had done everything possible to intensify this hysteria, because it could be only useful to him. He had strange, half-involuntary helpers. For instance, the "Tatkreis," a group of men associated with the magazine *Die Tat* who released the slogan: Responsible young Germans no longer dare render any services to the Weimar Republic—the "new" is marching in. When the "new" had arrived, the leaders of this group were quickly rendered impotent.

On that 30th of January 1933, not only the National Socialists but also other rightist organizations, for example, the Steel Helmet, took part in a torchlight parade honoring the new chancellor and Hindenburg, who had appointed him. These other organizations were eliminated within a few months.

The Reichstag building was set on fire at the end of February, and the National Socialists installed their SA men as auxiliary police. A week later elections were held, and again the National Socialists received no majority. They only attained it with help of Hugenberg's party [German Nationalists]. Now a spectacle took place, that was the most insidious abuse of Prussian history. In the Garrison Church at Potsdam (dedicated to the memory of Frederick the Great) a ritual was performed that was meant to create a link with the past, with the so-called National Revolution—Hitler bowed before Hindenburg! Several days later the newly elected Reichstag presented the new chancellor with the Enabling Act; [4] the Communists were outlawed because they were instigators of the Reichstag fire; only the Social Democrats held out against the act. The middle-class parties all voted for it, the Democrats (now the State party) against the advice of Heuss, the Catholic Center against the advice of Brüning but under the influence of Monsignor Ludwig Kaas, who soon departed for Rome.

Everything appeared to be legal. Hitler had the power, and the parties that had helped him disappeared within a short time, even the party of the unfortunate Hugenberg. Papen was shorn of power, and he could be thankful that he was not murdered, as were his closest associates, on June 30, 1934.[5] Germany was split into two peoples. The one side cheered the Führer—the many young people who saw in him the political savior, and the ambitious who hoped to get power and to profit through him. In small universities the SA consisted of students who were prepared to sacrifice everything; in other places the SA consisted of strong-arm gangs who molested Jews, former Socialists, and Communists. The first concentration camp was established, mild as yet in comparison with the later ones; leftist politicians were the first to be penned up in them. They were later released, but under constraint of silence.

Chapter Seven

The Rule of Hitler

Any attempt to speak of the Germans after 1933 must be only tentative. The younger generation must constantly be reminded that Hitler did not have his many followers because he disclosed to them that he would lead them into the greatest war of all history and would then forsake them in the midst of their extreme misery. Nor did he reveal that he would kill millions of Jews.

If Germans are questioned today about the summer of 1933—all who are forty-five or older can talk about it— different versions of what happened will be told, dependent on the attitude of each person. And soon the nature of the dictatorship becomes apparent. No longer did one person know what another was experiencing. The breakdown began as early as 1933 and became more serious toward the outbreak of the war: telephones were tapped, the mail was censored, and informers were employed; by the time the war began it had developed to such an extent that Germany was divided into small cells. The foreign press was rarely admitted, and listening to foreign broadcasts was prohibited. No one could check the public news service.

As early as 1933 it was no longer possible for those who were of critical mind to speak with those who were enthusiasts. No one who only read German newspapers and listened to the

German radio could understand the criticism. To be sure, some courageous newspapers, even big local publications, still existed. But of necessity these had to phrase their criticisms, and often their sarcasm, so carefully that the enthusiasts did not even notice them. But they were forced to notice certain other things.

The first boycott of the Jews, on April 1, 1933, was a public affair and a repellent one. Yet no critical voice was heard; even the Christian churches did not officially protest. But at that time the excitement over the "seizure of power" and over Potsdam was still in the air. The next step was "political equalization." All parties except the National Socialist party were dissolved; the unions were all abolished the day after May 1st. In the more obstinate South German states the federal representatives, who had been sent to all states, carried out Hitler's orders.

And from then on, up to the war, everything proceeded in the same rhythm. They simply bluffed their way through, and if any action met with resistance the Führer declared that it had been done against his will. This advance and retreat depended also upon the climate of foreign affairs. When foreign reaction did not have to be taken into consideration, the policy became more radical; when the reaction abroad was unfavorable, the policy was to retreat. This can be said of the policy toward the Jews, toward the churches, toward the intellectuals, in fact toward all the remaining forms of independent life in the National Socialist state. Up to a certain point the same was to happen in the war but there, of course, completely subject to military considerations.

Large meetings, first of the rectors of German universities and then of the University of Heidelberg, were held in the town of Heidelberg in July 1943. Josef Goebbels and the minister of education, B. Rust, were present. At these meetings it was proclaimed that German science was to be protected—a step taken rather late by the Third Reich. What had preceded this decision? Through their technical knowledge the Allies had discovered methods to detect and destroy German submarines, even by night [radar], when they had to surface during their long-distance runs. Admiral Karl Dönitz [1] had noticed this, too late and after fantastic losses, and had succeeded in convincing Hitler that 5000 chemists and physicists must be recalled from the front, and that science in general had to be preserved. The result was the meeting at Heidelberg. In the morning Rust spoke very frankly to the rectors and to the professors of Heidelberg. He said that he had always warned against neglecting science, but that he no longer had access to the Führer. The consequence was that his speech, scheduled for the afternoon, was cancelled. Goebbels, who, after Hitler, was primarily responsible for the neglecting and gagging of science, spoke instead. He could always find the right key to an audience, and he changed his attitude as soon as he observed that he was not being interrupted by the usual applause. Once, however, applause did break out among the students in the gallery, when he spoke of the achievements of German research. Apart from the wounded, the student body at that time consisted mainly of women—only in the department of medicine were there men in uniform—it was from this corner that the applause came. As is well known, it was much too late by that time. You cannot strangle the spirit of scholarship for ten years, expel or execute the leading Jewish scholars, and then expect to restore everything with one single stroke. However that may be, the German university owes its survival to these measures; and the same protection was extended to other, non-scientific branches of learning.

Every absolute dictatorship has a policy that permits certain "islands of freedom" to exist. But no one can be certain what the morrow will bring. Anti-Jewish posters were removed from Berlin before the Olympic Games started in 1936, and American tourists praised the beautiful and obviously ambitious city—they saw nothing of the concentration camps.

How many Germans knew about them? This question is not easy to answer. Everyone knew, at least after 1938, that Jews as well as leftists were being persecuted in an inhuman manner. Anyone who denies this is lying. But most people could not possibly know the extent of these deeds. One thing must be kept in mind: Nowhere in the world were these occurrences brought up for open and reliable discussion. The British government was the first to issue a statement based upon information received from victims who had escaped; but this did not happen until after war had broken out in the fall of 1939, and naturally did not reach Germany. Those who knew about it, perhaps through the radio or from newspapers that had been smuggled in, could not make any use of this knowledge without endangering their lives. Even though the Americans at the denazification trials after 1945 were not willing to believe it, the truth is that the "little Nazis" knew less than anyone else about the atrocities that were committed in the name of the German people at a command from their Führer. Those of us who listened to forbidden foreign broadcasts knew more about these things, and naturally the higher-ranking members of the National Socialist party also knew enough. In those circles a wave of sadism prevailed. Consider the following: Enemy propaganda of World War I had accused Germany of atrocities that never really occurred. Hitler and his executors surpassed anything that anti-German propaganda had been able to invent. The actual National Socialist behavior outdid everything, and so corroborated everything of which Germany had been unjustly accused from 1914 to 1918.

I was Privatdozent at the University in Tübingen during those first years, and had just been appointed professor a semester before Hitler's ascension to power. Why did a large number of students in Tübingen also join the SA at that time? For one thing, the public pressure that was being exerted on all classes and age groups may also have had its effect on some, even on the younger ones. On the whole, however, it was more the result of a desire not to stand idly by in the general turmoil. "We march!" These words had a magical meaning. "Wir werden weiter marschieren, wenn alles in Scherben fällt, denn heute gehört uns Deutschland, und morgen die ganze Welt." ["We shall march on, even though everything goes to pieces, for today Germany belongs to us, and tomorrow, the whole world."] Later, for tactical reasons, it was changed to, "denn heute da hört uns Deutschland" ["for today Germany longs to hear us"]. The need for the "heroic" and military games and exercises—their attraction can hardly be understood today. In Tübingen, where only a handful of Jews could be found, antisemitism scarcely existed, at least not at the University. For that reason, many who became victims of propaganda were all the more ready to believe what was said about the alleged domination of the Jews in Berlin. Since there was little industry and therefore little Marxism, some people were all the more likely to believe what they heard about the Communists and the socialists. Another point attacked by the intellectual National Socialist youth was the influence of the clergy in politics, and to this day I can hear the group of young Catholic students who explained to me that they had joined the SA because they believed that they would thus also be doing their best for the church by freeing it from the false power hunger of some of their priests.

Though from the beginning the SA was always mentioned in the reports made by those who had been persecuted and tortured, one thing must be clarified: There were various kinds of SA units. Those who in the beginning behaved outrageously were usually not the young members but the old core of the SA who had long before won their spurs in street fights in Berlin. However, new units soon became involved in these atrocities too. For instance, the SA men of Tübingen were told to participate in a demonstration against the courageous Catholic Bishop of Rottenburg and to start a brawl in front of the bishop's palace. Many were passive, but it took real courage simply to walk away in uniform, and few of them could muster this courage; among the others, many at least felt ashamed. Then, in November 1938, because a young Jew had shot a German diplomat in Paris, the notorious pogrom was ordered: Jews were openly mistreated, Jewish homes plundered, and Jewish houses of worship destroyed. This happened also in Heidelberg. To the credit of the leaders of the local party in Heidelberg it must be said, however, that the sections of the city north of the Neckar escaped this destruction. But all those Jews who up to that time had not emigrated, because they did not have the opportunity, or because they enjoyed special protection as veterans of World War I, or because they simply could not imagine a life away from their German homeland were now particularly humiliated and mistreated. Incomprehensible things occurred— Goebbels later declared that these organized misdeeds were a spontaneous reaction of the people.

The campaign of National Socialism against the Jews and the Christian churches has generally been considered particularly abhorrent. Concerning this it should be said that before 1933 the campaign against the Jews had not always been an important feature in Hitlerite propaganda. When the economic crisis was being exploited, antisemitism was temporarily of little importance, and not only German half-Jews but Jews themselves had illusions about their fate after Hitler gained victory. Besides, Hitler's government did protect some Jews to the very end—Göring's secretary of state, for example, was a Jew. On the whole, however, not even before 1933 could illusions about Hitler's attitude toward the Jews be seriously entertained. Yet, no one, perhaps not even Hitler in his wildest dreams had any premonition regarding the orders he would give after 1939.

In contrast to this, the campaign against the churches could have been anticipated from the general brutalization of the National Socialist movement after 1930, though it could not be detected in the statements of its official program. One point in the party program, which for the most part contained vague generalities (typical of Hitler's smattering of education and especially typical of one of his colleagues) stated that the party was in favor of "positive Christianity." By 1933, however, Hitler and especially Goebbels were so far removed from organized Christianity that already then the churches could expect the worst to happen if they tried to resist the brutalization of the community and, in particular, the efforts to alienate the youth from the churches.

In the beginning the position of the churches was not quite clear. Hitler, at first, managed to make a deep incursion into the Evangelical church through the "German Christians," [2] whom he, not a Protestant, actually addressed over the radio before the church elections. These German Christians consisted of a variety of elements; by no means were all of them National Socialists; some were old liberals, who felt themselves forced into opposition because of certain trends toward orthodoxy that were being advocated in the state churches. Later, however, the group consisted of those National Socialists who, more or less obviously, wanted to bring the Evangelical church under subjugation to the Hitler regime. Individual national state churches resisted successfully, others steered a middle course. It can be said that on the whole a nucleus of ecclesiastic resistance was maintained not only by the so-called Confessional Church [3] but also by individual state churches until 1939. Those who know the Evangelical church today know that there are as yet aftereffects.[4]

Nor was the Catholic Church in Germany uniform in its reactions at first, although the response of the Roman Catholic Church as a whole was a bit different. Some of the leading bishops sympathized to a certain extent with Hitler and hoped to influence him. The Vatican was the first important foreign power to recognize Hitler by negotiating a concordat with him in the summer of 1933. Its purpose was, of course, not to support Hitler but to secure the rights of the Catholic Church in Germany. This attempt was only partly successful. The Vatican soon realized, after the concordat had been drawn up, that too much had optimistically been taken for granted under the influence of advisers who saw everything in too rosy a light. Later the Vatican followed a policy that attempted to protect the rights of the Church in Germany without causing open conflict. Courageous bishops like Count Clemens von Galen received obvious support from Rome even during the war. The Evangelical bishops received no such support from outside and yet some of them, such as Bishop Theophil Wurm of Württemberg, were particularly courageous.

In both churches some were fighting for freedom to do ministerial work and to preach, and they fought especially for their youth. The radical groups of the National Socialist party began to fight openly against Christianity itself. Whenever they went too far, it was said that the Führer had not known about it. This, by the way, was the soothing sentence used for all occasions: These are only the firebrands, the Führer thinks otherwise. Actually, Hitler was only the tactician, but inwardly, he was the hottest firebrand of them all, the fiercest hater, a man of the most elementary brutality.

There can be no doubt about the fact that in 1934 and 1935 the masses of the people were for him. He was successful in foreign affairs; in 1935 he abrogated the Versailles Treaty through the Anglo-German Naval Agreement,[5] and in 1933 he had already resigned from the League of Nations. German unemployment fell rapidly, military conscription was reestablished, huge national work projects, such as the construction of the super highways, provided employment, as did the rapidly increased and barely concealed rearmament.[6]

At the Nürnberg party congresses Hitler celebrated his triumphs before gigantic mass meetings. Tens of thousands of those assembled there were glowing idealists who were prepared to sacrifice everything for the movement. As for the in-between generation of that time, one must bear in mind that they labored under the impressions of their experiences in 1918, which many had not understood correctly. At that time they had had the feeling that the old ruling classes had failed and that on the other hand Germany had been betrayed by international socialism. Now, at last, a "community of the people as a whole" was to be created. This made it easy for many of them to ignore flaws that were evident even to them. They could not pierce through to the basically nihilistic point of view held by Hitler and his closest followers. What they saw was success in the foreign policy and progress in the economy; what they did not want to see was the persecution of the Jews and the churches. Actually, the Jews were not persecuted with open shamelessness until later, until November 1938.

Thus German boys and girls, members of the HJ and the BDM,[7] gaily traveled through the country; the Labor Service worked at improving the soil and at other generally useful jobs; and a German army arose once more. Because Hindenburg was still alive—though he no longer had any influence —the fact that all this was happening under the leadership whose very existence represented the darkest blot on German history was concealed. After Hindenburg's death in 1934, Hitler, in an obscure maneuver, managed to have himself declared Führer and chancellor of the Reich and above all had the army swear allegiance to him. Even after this, middle-class ministers still served in the cabinet, which, by the way, had not met for years even before the war. One of these ministers, the Catholic Baron Eltz von Rübenach, resigned from the cabinet upon refusing the "golden party emblem" because of his philosophical views. This must be considered one of the bravest acts of the National Socialist era.

Many opponents of the regime, even those who until then wanted nothing to do with the army, consistently placed their hopes on the Reichswehr—for the last time during the Jewish pogroms of 1938. But the Reichswehr had no political training. It was a superb army technically, but, wholly apart from the fact that they would have found no following among many younger officers and men, its leaders could not make up their minds to defy their oath in order to reject Hitler and make a constitutional state out of Germany again with the help of the troops. The customary accusations made after 1945, which make the Reichswehr the scapegoat, are in this connection unjust.

A modern totalitarian dictatorship can hardly be overthrown from within. Yet it generally becomes rapidly corrupt. At least since March 1936 even the so-called elections in which only a "yes" or "no" vote was possible were systematically falsified. Nevertheless, what I have said before, that the masses of the people were for Hitler, is true. The Reichstag had become nothing more than an agency of the party, as in Russia today, and acclaimed Hitler at every opportunity. The German people had no chance to express themselves, at all events not the considerable minority who looked on with growing apprehension. When I say that a great number of people stood behind Hitler, I must make certain distinctions. The masses stood behind his outward successes—the economic upsurge, which made itself felt in the decline of unemployment (though the real causes of this decline were not obvious), the stiffening of the foreign policy, the gradual release from the shackles of Versailles. Substantial segments of these masses could have been diverted from Hitler had it been possible to keep them better informed about Hitler's measures against the Jews and his attitude toward the churches. Though many were not interested in protecting the Jews or the churches, harsh details would have deterred them. The regime, however, used a method that has always had its effect upon the small-souled man: It made its opponents look despicable by showing pictures of them wearing the degrading clothes of prisoners. Not too many could resist feeling superior to the victims. But the main thing was that there were no means available for counter propaganda among the ranks of the would-be believers. The state controlled the news disseminating machinery and thus the topics that were for public discussion, just as is the case in the countries of the Eastern bloc today. Though the individual may himself remain free under a dictatorship, he is in a miserable position when he finds that he cannot help others in distress. Informers were everywhere, they destroyed friendships and families and broke up marriages. After the attempted murder of Hitler on July 20, 1944, the demand to denounce even one's closest friends and relatives was crassly restated and announced everywhere. Even the university had to submit to this shameful procedure.

Those who were ready to believe were at least at first in a state of mind that can be compared to religious faith. Even well-intentioned people usually would not listen to criticism. Those who wished to criticize had to produce evidence, and this could be dangerous without achieving anything. The well-intentioned ones could always point to the many followers of the regime, who in all good faith were prepared to make sacrifices for it.

Meanwhile the state of affairs around Hitler grew steadily worse; the yes men were pushing toward the top. In 1938 the leadership of the army was reorganized too, in a stroke that was not without criminal implications. In the meantime Joachim von Ribbentrop had become foreign minister. The government consisted of obedient amateurs, and Hitler found little if any resistance from those in his immediate surroundings. In the leadership of the party itself Martin Bormann gradually moved to the top over Hess, a weak man who was slowly becoming more abnormal. Bormann had the most radical convictions and was extremely brutal in matters relating to the Jews and the churches.[8]

In 1938 Austria was invaded and annexed, and "Greater Germany" was founded. The Austrians were taken by surprise—the government of Kurt von Schuschnigg was popular only with the Catholic People's party, the socialist workers had been suppressed, and the "Greater Germany" group was closely related to National Socialists—there was no resistance. A fact that has often been forgotten by Austrians since 1945 is that in many cities crowds stood ready to cheer Hitler or the German troops. Even the Austrian episcopate was divided. On the day of the German invasion I traveled from the Dolomites through Austria. The villages between Brenner and Innsbruck were deserted, because a devout Catholic population lived there and was hostile to Hitler. In Innsbruck a happy throng waited at the railroad station, and in the villages of the Inn valley enthusiasts could be seen, but nothing, naturally, was seen of the others.

After this success came the destruction of Czechoslovakia in October 1938—the territories in which German was spoken were annexed to Germany. In March 1939 the remainder of the country was occupied, and thus Hitler's claim that he wanted only German territory was proved a lie. Up to this point the West had looked on, had practically supported Hitler in September 1938, but now the mood changed. War was in the offing and broke out in September 1939, when Hitler attacked Poland. The Polish government had not handled things very ably, and then Hitler had invented stories of atrocities and had seized the broadcasting station at Gleiwitz by using Germans in Polish uniforms. England and France came to the defense of Poland—World War II had begun.

Chapter Eight

World War II

Psychologically, the German people were placed in a difficult situation by the war. Internal criticism of the regime had increased since 1938 in spite of Hitler's successful foreign policy.[1] Perhaps it is to the credit of the German middle class that the Jewish pogroms of November 1938 had evoked horror even among those Germans who were usually numbered among the so-called middle-class antisemites. And then, in August 1939, Hitler suddenly changed his attitude. In order to annihilate Poland he allied himself with the Soviet Union, which up to that time he had loathed.[2] What had become of the slogan, "Fight Communism"? Could one actually go on believing what this Führer said? Well, there certainly were enough Germans who simply wanted to believe and to obey—regardless of what it was they believed. With the help of the Bolsheviks, the direction now taken was against the West, against Versailles.

Here again a national nerve had been touched. Many officers and soldiers of World War I were recalled because the defeat, or the "injustice" of 1918 was to be rectified; and the young men, more or less enthusiastically, followed a Führer whom they could compare to no one because they knew no others. War with the outside world meant that national unity was, of course, a patriotic duty. At the same time Germany was cut off from foreign countries; foreign newspapers were practically unobtainable, except for a few that were considered harmless; listening to foreign radio broadcasts was prohibited and was now severely punished, even by death. And, also at the same time, the churches were prevented from sending the local papers to members of their congregations who had been drafted. The Warthe [3] region that had been taken away from Poland was organized along completely anti-Christian lines—a good example of how Hitler would proceed in Germany once he had won the war.

But in Germany people knew little about all this. What was known was that millions of Germans soldiers were in the field —and all Germans wished them a safe return. Among those soldiers were many who inwardly were almost being smothered by National Socialism. That these, who did not believe in Hitler, had to die because of him is a tragedy of German history. "Für Führer, Volk und Vaterland" ["For the Führer, the People, and the Fatherland"], so ran the formula for obituary notices, and the first part of this was indeed the awful truth—they had died for Adolf Hitler.

This man, who in *Mein Kampf* had made a laughing stock of the German leadership of World War I, now made more mistakes than they had made. He had no conception of the world outside Germany, and he spoke no foreign language.

At first the war seemed to progress according to his predictions. France was overrun, and he hoped for an easy victory over England. But he had badly underestimated the latter. In the decisive period of 1940–41 the British fought alone, even in Africa. There the Italians, who had entered the war after the collapse of France, met with continual reverses until the Germans, under Rommel, came to their rescue.[4]

Hitler brought about his own downfall when he attacked Russia in 1941 and then in the same year declared war on the United States. In a tactless and childish maneuver he publicly made fun of Churchill and Roosevelt, but he had a certain amount of respect for Stalin, whose personality closely resembled his own. Indeed, he avidly imitated more of the methods used by the Bolshevik regime.[5] In general, National Socialism discarded more and more of the basic ideas that had been the foundation of its propaganda.

When Hitler finally realized that he had brought his people to the brink of ruin, he repeatedly stated that the nation had not been obedient enough, and that it therefore deserved to perish. Thus even his feelings for Germany did not subdue his injured pride, and in the end he cared only about himself and his power. He had only used the German people as an instrument to obtain power; when he had worn out this instrument he cast it aside.

But this must not tempt us to be one-sided. The people fought courageously and suffered courageously even under Hitler. After the war naive foreigners often asked why more Germans had not defected to the enemy once they had recognized their Führer's madness. Because he is concerned for the safety of his comrades, a soldier very rarely deserts for political reasons. Once he is in the enemy's hands he will be questioned about his unit, and thus runs the risk of endangering the lives of his comrades. It is easy for foreigners and German theorists to point out constantly to the Germans that all these soldiers actually did fight for Hitler. Naturally they did. What alternative did they have? Especially when faced with an enemy in the West who did not understand the problems involved in German resistance. Only the Russians formed a nucleus of opposition among the German prisoners—simple to do under a dictatorship—but they did not do it in order to help the Germans ease their conscience about Hitler.

With this we come to the most delicate question of all—opposition to the Hitler regime during the war.[6] Even before the war cells of resistance had existed, but the majority of the people had shown no interest in such efforts. That there was resistance became widely known only when a few brave men attempted to assassinate Hitler and to stage an uprising on

July 20, 1944. These men were aware of the fact that after they had vanquished Hitler they would have to lead the German people through a military defeat that Hitler had brought upon them. Some of these men were immediately executed; among them was Count Claus Schenk von Stauffenberg,[7] who died exclaiming "Long live our holy Germany!" The majority were held captive for a long time. They were tortured and then put to death in the most degrading fashion. A number of them were secretly assassinated just a few days before the end of the war. These men deserve admiration. They rose against a reality that was almost unconquerable, both from within and from without, and sacrificed their lives for Germany.

Today the problem connected with the resistance is often oversimplified by people who up to 1945 rejected any thought of opposition. This is dangerous. It must be understood that many Germans were against assassinating Hitler in the middle of a war, and we must understand that a young lieutenant at the Russian front who, perhaps, had been brought up with the Hitler Youth was horrified by the reports of the deed of July 20th. Any absolute assertions about the resistance must result in historical bias.

Let us return to the theme of the German people and their history. Until 1933 public opinion existed in Germany. It could be gauged and its basic outline established. In 1933, however, public opinion was suppressed, but in many ways it was still possible to evaluate the nation. In 1939, with the outbreak of the war, these ways were closed. From then on, memory tells us that even private conversations were hardly ever really frank, except among very small groups. All criticism was punishable by death because it undermined the will to fight. This was very effective at a time when people were torn from their normal environment and placed in completely new surroundings (civil defense, compulsory war work, evacuation, and others). A young person in West Germany today cannot imagine what it meant for two people to meet for the first time under such circumstances, because human contact at that time involved also one's political attitude. And how different the experiences of each person were. One had been in Russia for years, the other in Africa, the third at sea in a submarine, the fourth in a city that was slowly but surely being demolished by bombs, the fifth in a munitions factory, the sixth in a concentration camp, and the seventh an emigrant in a foreign country that was at war with his homeland.

These emigrants became citizens of the foreign countries at that time or later, at least, most of them did. Even among those, destiny erected walls of separation. Some had good fortune in the country they had adopted, others had come to a country that assimilated foreigners with difficulty; some already understood the foreign language, others had the difficult task of learning a new language in their old age; some lost the entire part of their family that had not escaped from Germany, others knew that members of their family had been saved; some maintained their connections with German culture, others made a complete break with the past and began a new life; some were embittered and remained embittered, others sooner or later after 1945 returned to their old homeland. Some worked hard for Germany after 1945, either from abroad or after coming back.[8]

Thus, because of Hitler and the war, the German nation had become a mass of people who now scarcely communicated openly with each other. In order to understand this lack of communication it would be helpful to have spent a night in an air-raid shelter during an attack upon a large city, or to have been in one of the overcrowded trains that groped their way through completely destroyed railroad stations. Apathetic silence reigned; occasionally a few disgruntled words were heard, but now and again the desire to help flickered up.

Those who have not lived under a dictatorship cannot grasp how important the political joke can be at such times. So much so, that sometimes the more harmless ones were known even to some of the ruling group. On the other hand, a large group of less important henchmen know no jokes, and, of course, are never told any. For the young readers I have chosen two examples from among thousands. The first probably originated in Fascist Italy and was then translated. A good fairy gave Germans three attributes: to be honest, intelligent, and National Socialists. But an evil fairy objected and declared that one person could only have a choice of two attributes. Therefore a German could be intelligent and a National Socialist, but not honest as well; or honest and a National Socialist, but not intelligent as well; or honest and intelligent, but not a National Socialist as well. This was on the lighter side. Now one from the war that belongs to the macabre. During the annihilation of Jews in Poland a drunken SS [9] company commander said to a Jew: "I have a glass eye. I will not kill you if you can identify it." The Jew examined him and said, "The left one." "True, but how did you know?" "It had a kindly light in it, sir!"

For the troops in the field the situation was not like that at home. No informers lurked behind every group, and men were not too much under the pressure of politics and the Gestapo.[10] Here only duress from the outside existed. What the German soldiers endured in World War II has hardly been equaled. It can, perhaps, be compared to the sufferings of the armies defeated by the Germans in the same war; but those sufferings were of shorter duration, except in the case of the Russians. The defamation of German soldiers that was rife not only in foreign countries but also to a certain extent in Germany after 1945 was unjust. Many of the soldiers had no intimation of the acts of cruelty the SS was perpetrating behind them while they were fighting, or that their bravery was being besmirched by those mass exterminations with which such men as Himmler, Heydrich, and Eichmann are connected.

In Germany itself there were many who had no inkling of these atrocities, and there were always instances of voluntary self-sacrifice—I recall, for instance, how hard our wounded students and women students worked in order to be able to continue their studies and with what eagerness they pursued them.

Let me speak about the German university. Here, as in all fields of endeavor, there were those who were members of the National Socialist party and those who were not. But that was not indicative of the real border line of political viewpoints and human decency.[11] In addition numerous more or less political organizations were established by professors and by students. If all the members of the political organizations had wholeheartedly been in favor of Hitler's goals—in this case this means in favor of making the universities more political and more radical—the German university would have gone out of existence before 1939. But that was not the case. We who did not join the National Socialist party or, rather, who explicitly refused to join, would not have been in a position to continue lecturing if we had not continuously been protected by members of the National Socialist party and by the political organizations—both by the professors and by the students. Here again, just as much is being wrongly oversimplified today as was oversimplified by the Americans during the denazification trials after 1945, with which I shall deal later.

Among the professors as well as among the students there were fanatical "fighters for the Führer," but they practically formed an island to which the other university members sought no access. Among the professors these radicals formed a small group. Not even the leader of the National Socialist Dozentenbund [Lecturers' Union], who did much to protect those whose opinions were different from his own, belonged to this group. At most German universities the professors who were the most prominent National Socialists had first been appointed in 1933; only a few of the older professors joined the radical camp. In the middle, between us and the radicals, was a heterogeneous group of which the majority were irreproachable in their lectures as well as in their research. I can well remember the surprise of some students coming from radical schools to hear lectures that were similar to the ones given today.[12]

Many students who came to the university at the beginning of the war were less perturbed than the students who came immediately after 1933, because they had practically grown up with National Socialism. After 1940 women students predominated. Their political affiliation provided, in Heidelberg at least, protection for the university. This political youth, in its best representatives, fought every form of pettiness and malice, and therefore frequently clashed with other sections of their party. They took a severely critical attitude, and after the beginning of the war saw some of the male student leaders hang around at home, instead of going into the army, because political duties sheltered them—in many cases these later became political supervisors of the military staff. Of these groups a greater percentage survived the war than was the average for male students.

It was deeply affecting to see the ideals of the idealists gradually crumble. People abroad accuse Germans of forsaking Hitler only when it became evident that he had lost the war. This was not true of those young people I knew, nor of the group of generals who joined the conspiracy. Our students became indignant as soon as they began to realize that during the war an ever-increasing persecution of the Jews was taking place. To be sure, it was rather moderate as far as people knew in Germany—at least moderate in comparison to the mass executions in Poland and then in Russia. But the bulk of the people in Germany could know nothing of these until the war was over.

The awful thing about this war, which also characterized the dictatorship, was that as the fighting at the front grew harder (harder partly because of the mistakes made by the "mulishly" stubborn leadership of the Führer), the brutality within Germany and in the occupied territories became more flagrant. But for no one, not even for the most critical of Hitler's enemies, was it possible to see the situation as a whole. The individual could always see only limited sections of it. Nor could the individual possibly judge how much was or was not exaggeration in the rumors that were circulating. For example, the report that Hitler chewed rugs in fits of temper was not true. Among others, rumors circulated about deeds of violence that had never been committed.

When the enemy invasion in the West began on June 6, 1944, and the fighting in the East grew more desperate, the conditions at home were already very bad. The enemy's superiority in the air, which extended even over Germany, was steadily increasing and the air raids became more gruesome. Hitler, who had claimed that he would destroy all London by air—"erase" it in fact—had for several years now not been able to attack London or England. Instead he sat all night long by the radio in order to follow the reports of the flight of enemy planes over Germany. Life in the large cities became simple hell. In Heidelberg the noise made by the hail of bombs that crashed down upon Mannheim and Ludwigshafen went on for hours; by comparison, very little happened to Heidelberg, and that practically only when the front had moved so close that the enemy in their attempt to stop rail traffic also hit houses in the vicinity of the railroad station. My last lecture in the winter semester of 1944–45 was held in the auditorium of the Zoological Institute because our building was no longer being heated. When a single airplane attacked, only an alert was sounded and the lecture, which was held on the top floor, continued. I can still see the heads of those taking notes duck down one after the other as an airplane attacked the railroad 100 meters away and we heard the bombs fall. The students continued to work hard, aware of the fact that every hour spent with the books was a gain.

In the fall of 1944 the Allies pushed forward onto German

soil at Aachen; in January 1945 the Russians began their offensive on old German territory. Dreadful tales were told of the suffering of the German population in the East, a region which up to that time had been under the strictest control of the National Socialist party. The district leader of East Prussia, Koch, had forbidden all attempts at escape, but then he himself had retreated at a convenient time. The roads of North Germany were jammed with the overloaded carts of refugees; some, like Bismarck's daughter-in-law, remained in Varzin, and the last that was heard about her and about the others was that they had been mistreated and killed. This was the so-called liberation of the East—one system of terror replaced another as a concomitant of bloody conquest. Now for the first time since Napoleon I, large areas of German territory became the battlefield of foreign armies and the stage for a terrible military collapse. In the West enemy troops were at least not systematically cruel, but the war there was perhaps even harder than in the East.

On April 30, 1945 the Führer committed suicide in Berlin. He had up to the very end maneuvered armies that no longer existed; the master liar had become the victim of his own lies. Goebbels also killed himself and his family. Bormann disappeared, and up to the present time the place where he is supposed to have died cannot be definitely identified. Göring and Himmler had already deserted Hitler and had attempted to reach an understanding with the enemy. Before his suicide Hitler had designated Admiral Dönitz as his successor, an admiral who had pathetically little political understanding, as he showed only too embarrassingly in his memoirs. On the 7th and 8th of May the armistice was signed. Nothing remained of the glory, of the dreams and the hopes of the Third Reich, all that was left were ruins and mass graves, and the terrible disappointment of all those who had been ardent believers to the very end. The Führer had forsaken them—by committing suicide; at first a false report had said that he had fallen in battle. His closest associates, Himmler and Göring, had betrayed him, and the miracle weapons that up to the very last had been announced had failed to appear. The attitude of never yielding in spite of everything, the attitude which diehards emphasized, was seldom evident. Only they clung to their old faith and concerned themselves neither about the Right nor the Left; for them Hitler had vanished in the manner of Barbarossa.

The last German troops had returned wearily through Heidelberg; they had hardly any weapons but still put up some resistance. The heads of the National Socialist party had long departed. The Americans came in 1945, on Good Friday.

In the general misery—everyone was worried about food, shelter (the occupying troops commandeered it), clothing, and the fate of the prisoners and the missing—the desire to know the meaning of what had happened was forced into the background; soon, however, it appeared again. And it was not the worst among the old Hitler adherents who asked themselves and others: "Was everything wrong, was everything meaningless?" Of course most people forgot for the time being what they had idolized, and because of the political housecleaning, that is, the removal of National Socialists from the administration and from other places of power, the search for the meaning and significance of those twelve years ended in a hopeless tangle.

No one who survived the twelve years in Germany had the right to a pharisaical attitude unless he had risked his life to fight the terrorizers. Even Karl Jaspers said at the time, "We are all guilty, why didn't we cry out against the injustice in the streets?" But soon it became quite clear that there were quite a few pharisees, and these had, in part, a pernicious influence on the American policy of denazification. A fact that has not been recognized or has been left out of stereotyped books and movies about the National Socialist period is that there were well-meaning and unselfish persons among the

National Socialist officials and Hitler Youth leaders. Many of them made considerable sacrifices for what they believed to be a good cause and the salvation of Germany. And during the war many who were inclined to be critical put aside their criticism because they considered that to be their duty as Germans. Only a platitudinous judgment that does not take into account historical reality can possibly forget this.

Hitler himself in the earliest days may actually have believed in his ideals, of course in the limited, fanatically egocentric form that was characteristic of him, and with the brutality toward other people, in part a result of insecurity, which such fanatics often show. He lacked the sensitivity and refinement that, for instance, Bismarck possessed. He did not appreciate many aspects of the German character. Actually, he hated some of these traits because he believed they were to blame for the German weakness of the last few centuries. The intellectual made him uneasy, which is why he hated the general staff. People were only instruments for him, and whenever he spoke of loyalty it reeked of false sentimentality. Apart from Goebbels, not one of the old National Socialist leaders remained loyal to him to the end. The National Socialist movement, which so often made use of the word "loyalty" in its slogans, showed no personal loyalty at its summit.

What had become of the National Socialism whose very name had been charged with power? The *National:* Well, we have seen that Hitler wished for the destruction of his people because they did not give him full support during his later insanity. The *Socialism:* Hitler gave the workers bread and games, but never since the end of the nineteenth century had the German working class been so politically helpless as under Hitler. No strike could be attempted because Hitler needed the productivity of industry. And in social questions he was on the side of the big industrialists, some of whom had helped him to survive the last crisis in 1932. What had become of the Nordic and the Germanic? In practice it had proved to be empty talk. Naked power was the core; everything else was propaganda used to hide that fact. Because of bad leadership many hundreds of thousands of German soldiers were sacrificed unnecessarily, especially in Russia, and millions of Jews were killed in mass extermination camps and by mass shootings. One more thing should be noticed: Many people, even the National Socialists, had blamed the last Kaiser for not dying in battle, and for running off to Holland. None of the Nazi leaders died in battle fighting the enemy; perhaps Bormann did, in the attempt to escape from Berlin in the last days. All talk about loyalty and heroism proved in the face of reality to be mere talk.

The balance remains negative. But all cannot yet be finally summed up, for with the year 1945 we come into our immediate present. We have no right to pass judgment on the past without taking into account how we are solving our own problems. Thus we cannot separate what we do from what we say about the past. Both make us what we are.[13]

Chapter Nine

From 1945 until 1961

Let us recall the words that had been written to Max Weber after 1918: "The German people now need an educator who can teach them to make something out of their experiences." But at this point something else Weber said calls for attention—in 1918 he had warned against the exaggerated confession of guilt by the Germans. The situation in 1945, however, was different; monstrous things had happened. The need for self-examination stood in the forefront, but even this time it was not a completely straightforward self-examination, because not all those who felt called upon to pronounce judgment were really qualified to do so, neither abroad nor at home. The period after 1933 had revealed some evil traces in the German picture, more than even pessimists had previously considered possible. And yet even here one should not make generalizations, because the public and the people abroad knew nothing of the many quiet deeds of decency and of neighborly love performed during the reign of terror. Of course, much remains that is painful and that even now has not been obliterated or eliminated from everyday life in Germany.

But this presentation and this point of view are exposed to the danger of being censured for forgetting that foreign countries were also responsible, and that this responsibility began when Russia and France pushed toward war in 1914; when the victors of 1918 misused their power; when these same victors let Hitler achieve results in foreign affairs after 1933 that they had denied to the Weimar Republic; when after 1945 they condemned the whole German people; and when the Western powers allowed Bolshevik Russia to bring terrorist methods deep into Germany and to sit in judgment of the accused Germans at the Nürnberg trials.

These are certainly factors that are more or less significant, but none of them dictated the conduct of the German people. That the Germans did not learn anything from the events of 1918 was not the fault of foreign countries. After 1925 the victors of World War I had softened toward Germany, and they could not be blamed for the fact that Hitler came after Stresemann and Brüning and abused their lenient policy. After 1945 the Allies believed Hitler's assertion that the whole German nation had been enthusiastic National Socialists. And the fact that the Russians came to Germany can, after all, be traced to Hitler's attack upon them. None of these things should be minimized, but one must really see both sides; not one of the factors just mentioned relieves the Germans of their responsibility—it is a paradox that some of the proudest Germans act as if the behavior of the German people always depended upon foreigners.

Of course, if influences from outside Germany were ever of importance, they were so in 1945 and have been ever since. A German state no longer existed, and the occupying powers had also taken over all formal authority. They exercised it in various ways and, to a certain extent, are still doing so. The Russians in the East and in Central Germany attempted and are still attempting with all their might to establish a Communist structure regardless of the opinion of the population, who, furthermore, had suffered terribly at the hands of their troops during the invasion and during the period that immediately followed.[1]

The Western occupation forces were more similar to each other than any of them were to the Russians. The French invasion was occasionally accompanied by unfortunate occurrences and afterward the economy of the French zone did not recover for a long time. The French hardly attempted to affect the German system of education, except that, like the Russians, they required that their language be taught everywhere. The English intervened in public administration rather strongly, and were still dismantling factories when the German economy in the American zone was beginning to thrive again. But, like the French, they soon refrained from eliminating former National Socialists.

The Americans were the determining power in the West.[2] They came to a country that was essentially unfamiliar to them. The economy, and at first this simply meant the providing of food, progressed most rapidly in their zone, but they intervened most actively in the life of the Germans. They considered it their particular task to eliminate the National Socialists. The word "to denazify" originated with them. Here they operated with conceptions that by no means corresponded with the actual nature of the dictatorship they were trying to destroy, and this is where they made their greatest mistakes. The American occupation policy was strict at the beginning, guided in part by ideas of the infamous Morgenthau Plan.[3] The Americans were especially distrustful of the German system of higher education and tried to find the origin of reactionary forces as well as of National Socialism. Many Americans failed to recognize the difference between the two, just as they did not know, for example, that the French system of education was and is much more conservative than the German. In many respects the Americans, without knowing it, started off with conceptions that were close to those of the National Socialist Teachers Association. This must be mentioned because that policy stirred up strong opposition among educated Germans, many of whom, however, only manifested that after the actual rule of occupation was over. In the field of education, which includes the universities, the American occupation policy combined two basic errors. One was that they failed to understand the German education system, the other was that they did not grasp correctly the inherent possibilities of the so-called denazification.

Before criticism is expressed, another statement must be made. The Americans had not asked for the assignment. Hitler had declared war on them, and in May 1945, even with the best intentions, no German government could have been found that was able to represent the Germans. The problem of eliminating the leading National Socialists would always have existed and would always have been difficult, even if it had been handled by independent Germans.

In other matters the Americans turned out to be most helpful. As far as the German people were concerned the hardest thing to bear, aside from the denazification, was the commandeering of apartments. By way of comparison an attempt should be made to study from the bottom up the effects a German occupation of a foreign country had on the people involved—the German occupation of Belgium during World War I, for instance—only then can one reach a judgment.

Soon American packages came pouring into Germany. Often they were gifts from people who lived far more regular lives than the German recipients had until that point been accustomed to. It would be interesting to draw a comparison between American help given to Germany at that time and the help Germans are giving their compatriots in the East zone today. After all, with the help they gave, the Americans did succeed in putting German economy back on its feet.

But the Americans were proceeding with fundamentally contradictory ideas. Their intention was to turn the Germans into a democratic nation again, but they claimed to want the support of the so-called democratic segments and to eliminate the National Socialists on the one hand, and on the other they continued to reject the German nation as a whole because they considered them all Hitlerites. Thus, because the Americans followed a mechanical method of denazification that embittered a large number of Germans, they jeopardized the successful realization of their main goal—the creation of a democracy in Germany. And thus, by failing to consider the opinions of German anti-Hitlerites, they weakened the prestige of these Germans, which in 1945 was very high among the German people.

So we come to the Germans themselves. In 1945 the Germans lived among ruins, among the ruins of their homes and, many of them, among the ruins of their beliefs. Food was obtained with difficulty; many hardly had a roof to cover their heads; many did not know whether their closest relatives were still alive or what had become of their soldiers. With the end of National Socialism the deep skepticism that had previously existed among the opponents of the Hitler regime became more widespread. An officer, and this is typical, had already written in 1943: "All that remains is simply to form one's own circle—in the family and in the home—in which the old culture can be preserved. Here as many of the cultural and spiritual values as possible must be introduced from the past." [4]

In 1945 many were more optimistic than that, especially those who had not been soldiers who had to fight for Hitler, and those who had long been critical of his regime. The very fact that they had survived was a reason for hope. How often did we say: "If we can only survive!" The ones who themselves belonged to the persecuted had even more right to say that. But at first our hands were empty, and the influence, even of those who had been dispossessed by the National Socialists, was for the time being very slight. People who had helped us survive were being arrested by the occupation forces.

In that summer of 1945 hardly any National Socialists were left among the German people. There were, of course, some who stubbornly held on to what had been, and who wished to know nothing of all that was being revealed. They were probably not too intelligent, but they had a certain conception of loyalty (a conception that had not been important to the old National Socialist leadership) to which they still clung. But many former National Socialists were now prepared one way or another for something new; most of them tried to digest what they had lived through, and some vied with one another in open confessions of guilt. All depended now upon whether the new order of things would prove so reliable that these people would support a new form of government.

The mistake made by the American military government in the denazification proceedings tribunals, which were virtually appointed by the Americans, was that first of all far too many people were punished, and then, that too many were removed from office. Proper perspective was completely lacking, and so was wholesome commonsense, of which the Anglo-Saxons have always been so proud. Of course it must be said in their defense that their task was completely without precedent. When the law that set up the German tribunals in the spring of 1946 began to take effect, one more injustice became evident.[5] The men who were the first to be brought before these tribunals were, for the most part, sorely needed at their administrative posts and in their businesses because they were trusted and considered to have political judgment. But these very cases were treated with the full severity of the law, in the first flush of enthusiasm and because of the charged atmosphere of the times. Others, who were not wanted anywhere by anybody, were allowed to wait and later were treated quite moderately because of the different climate of opinion. This was the worst mistake made by the denazification proceedings.

The National Socialists had at one time fought against the system prevalent during the Weimar Republic that rewarded party loyalty with promotion. But under National Socialism this very system had become firmly established, and the performance of those in public service declined rapidly because advancement was now completely controlled by politics. Even at the universities the National Socialists had introduced the "leadership principle" and thus had destroyed academic self-government. The result was that after 1935 a predominant number of the rectors and deans at German institutions of higher education owed their positions to National Socialism. In spite of this, every new appointment was fought over in most of the faculties, and in general, respectable standards were maintained. This speaks well for many of the men in charge of university affairs at the various ministries. The fact that political student leaders had the right to participate in filling vacancies was extremely dangerous—every dictatorship brings such a right into operation.

The German tribunals had to deal with this complicated situation as a whole and with the universities in particular. The danger here lay in the possibility that some people would be unjustly convicted and lay also, in a more general sense, in the possibility that the attitude toward the past twelve years would become confused as a result of the conflict arising from the exoneration of individuals while the people as a whole stood condemned. Thus "overcoming the past" began with frenzied fervor and with the wrong prognosis. The first ones to preside over and to participate in the German tribunals had been chosen with care, but they were inclined to theorize. When I, at that time the Prorector, pointed out at an open session that we who had not been members of the National Socialist party had survived through the secret support of members, the chairman of the court objected to this.[6]

Nevertheless, as I have said, the first months with all their difficulties were a time of hope. Those who were present will recall how the students came half-starved and in tattered uniforms to the university to inquire about the beginning of the lectures. These students were among the best we ever had (as the students had been during the war), and the suspicions the Americans had of them were quite unfounded. They worked hard and tenaciously, and in addition had to come to terms inwardly with the past and the present. This they did with the help of those among their teachers they believed had followed a straight course both before and after 1945.

It was a time of hope, but also a time of uncertainty and want. People were on the move everywhere; many simply wanted to return home; others no longer had a home—among them children who at 15 had been sent away somewhere. The people on the trains sat in brooding silence until a conversation began somehow, and experiences were related and questions flowed freely back and forth. But National Socialism itself was a long way away and was as dead as if these people had never known anything about it. The mass of people encamped in the open fields, ate scraps of bread, smoked the few cigarettes available (they sold at high prices), and crowded into the few trains still running. This was all that was left of a people who had once sung "Today Germany . . . tomorrow the whole world," a people who had been informed in 1940 that they were now the rulers of Europe.

Certainly hope existed, but so did many heavy burdens! The heaviest was that Hitler's attack upon Russia had brought Bolshevism to Germany, where a state of officials and of party bosses was formed. Today the Germans in the West cannot speak for the Germans in the East. Though they had not supported National Socialism more than those in the West, they are atoning for all the Germans by having to live for nearly thirty years under a dictatorship, sixteen of them under that of the Russians.

More can be said about the West, but that actually consists only of what we Germans in the West have endured. Even the younger people have lived under the shadow of 1945, or have at least been conscious of it. This shadow has still not been dissipated.

There are many whose fate is not known to this day—that of soldiers in Russia as well as of German refugees from the

Eastern regions. Pictures of those being sought are still circulated in the refugee camps and at meetings of the displaced, and the question asked whether anybody knows anything of the person shown there. The German people, once such lovers of order, had to experience the disintegration of order at the end of Hitler's war in a matter that is of the greatest importance to all nations—the records of the fates of people.

In the mass-extermination camps of the SS, millions had been wiped out; around 1945 this contempt for people—the Germans had once considered it the way in which to identify other races—boomeranged. But, unfortunately, not in a consistent manner. The suffering the German people have endured as a consequence of the Hitler regime has been unfair, not at all matched to the part taken in the dictatorship and the advantages gained from it.

In conclusion, I should like to discuss other similar disparities of the German people, of course not in historical retrospect but nevertheless seen in the total historical perspective, so that those who live through these times can see them clearly. The real discord in German life today is between the situation and the mood that existed after 1945 and the reality of the present. First of all, the external facts: No one who walked through the ruined German cities could have anticipated that fifteen years later nearly everything would be rebuilt and that West Germany would have become one of the leading industrial countries of the world; that unemployment would no longer exist, but rather a shortage of workers; and that the great majority of people would have a good income. Even most of the refugees from former German territories or from areas colonized by Germans in the East have been included in this process, though not exactly on the same level as the old inhabitants of the West. This is a part of the inequality I have mentioned.

Moreover, no one in 1945 could have dreamed that West Germany would soon be so important as a state. This has even been recognized recently in a Soviet memorandum, in which the Soviet Union and the Federal Republic were designated the greatest states of Europe. Thus, great success was achieved in the economic sphere and in foreign relations, at least from the outward view. But how do these triumphs relate to the German situation of 1945, to German ideas and hopes of that time?

In the first place, these successes have been achieved only by the West Germans. The natural wish of most Germans, that what was left of a sectioned Germany might be united, was among those wishes that have not been fulfilled. This is where the boundary of the success in foreign relations is reached.

A sad boundary indeed. No doubt it is connected with the fact that the successes have been achieved in the West. Opinions differ as to the question whether this boundary was unavoidable. To this day neither of the two opinions (the division of Germany could have been avoided, that is, eliminated, or it could not have been) can be substantiated with any certainty.

But one thing is certain, and again I must bring up the inequality in the distribution of the suffering with which Germans have had to atone for Hitler, people in the West have sometimes taken the fact too lightly in its ideological sense, that they are freer than the people in Central or in East Germany. All that was emphasized about Roman and Carolingian traditions during the talks between Cologne, Bonn, and Augsburg in and after 1950 was as unhistorical as it was pharisaical. To this must be added the ease with which Prussian history on the Rhine was ignored not merely by the leftists but also by the Christian side. A Communist editor in Heidelberg once commented upon the fall of Prussia in ten venomous lines, and some writers from the Rhineland did not need many more. I hold strongly to the view that the inequality with which the Germans have had to endure the catastrophies that have occurred since 1933 and also 1945 is a governing factor in the

relationship between the German past and the German present, even if those who are gainers by this inequality speak
little about it.

In 1918 people often spoke about the "war generation."
What did the war generation of 1945 feel and think? The
soldiers came home with a horror of war and military service
—even the good soldiers, in fact, principally these. They had
had to learn that even the greatest bravery could not change
the course of destiny. Others had considered the misuse of the
German soldiery by the political leadership of the National
Socialists a disgrace. Many others would also have denounced
military service under other circumstances, as Remarque did
after World War I. All of these were now exposed to the
influence of German education and the reeducation by the
victors in the West. This indoctrination concentrated, among
other things, upon telling young Germans, "You may never
again become soldiers." In fact, the German soldier was defamed in many circles in Germany and abroad. I have already
established this to have been an injustice. Many of you can
imagine the shock felt around 1950 after the "cold war" had
begun, when all this was suddenly forgotten, and the same
young Germans, or at least their younger brothers, were told
that it was now their duty to defend the West. This shock is
still having its effect today.

The "war generation" returned home with another basic
feeling, praise of comradeship. Much had become endurable
only because the unit, "the gang," had stuck together. I
would not speak about socialism, but a tendency to head in
that direction existed, because this was the only experience
that in any way resembled what the National Socialist leadership had taught, even though on the whole it had never lived
up to its teachings.

After the founding of the West German state in 1949, the
German economic policy was directed toward what consequently became the open market system and achieved results

that are well known. This caused some difficulties among the younger generation, but it seems evident to me that an open market economy, if it is carried through efficiently, and if certain regulations are made in the interest of the general public, does not necessarily contradict the principles of the "war generation." But what does cause complications is that this open market economy has been severely watered down through the influence exerted by the unions of pressure groups.

With this I return to the questions whose significance for the period around 1918 I have already discussed. How successful has the new form of government been? To what degree has it been able to penetrate to the awareness of the people? Has the nation accepted the far-reaching system of parliamentary democracy?

I cannot answer these questions; I can only make a few remarks. The German constitution, the Grundgesetz, was conceived under two influences—that of the last years of the Weimar Republic and that of National Socialism. This is a most interesting example of how events that have just ceased being living reality and have become recorded history leave aftereffects. But the discussions that were of such importance in the middle 1920s in the Weimar Republic have been neglected. The multiparty system has been redirected (by the Five Percent Clause and by the requirement that a majority attempting to unseat the chancellor must present another candidate), and an effort has been made to protect the individual from the state. The Grundgesetz is often attacked, but as long as its form and its content are adhered to, it is all right. When, however, its purport is infringed upon by those in high places, as was the case in the last presidential election, then it is endangered.

A specifically German problem is the relationship between bureaucracy and parliament; the general problem of contemporary democracy is how to protect a functioning democracy from one-sided commercial interests. The German bureaucracy today in comparison with the German parliament is stronger than the Grundgesetz intended or specified. The huge ministerial bureaucracy is the most powerful agency within the state's domain. This has advantages and disadvantages. It has the disadvantage that the German parliament proceeds more slowly and less efficiently under such conditions than had been intended. The parliamentary system is more firmly established today than it was in 1918, but it is not reflected in the way of life of the whole nation as are the parliamentary systems in England and the United States. In the Anglo-Saxon countries parliament functions according to laws that include the whole community, whereas in Germany it is an exception.

The year 1948 was a turning point in Germany's most recent history. From 1948 to about 1958 Germany's economy experienced a remarkable recovery and large segments of the nation satisfied their need to make up for lost time and acquire riches and happiness. In 1948 "overcoming the past," as it was later called, seemed to have been accomplished. But it was not accomplished, whatever the individual achievement may have been. The leading politicians, however, now no longer concerned themselves about it, because they were preoccupied with everyday tasks, and because they, in part, belonged to a generation that could not grasp the fact that for all Germans born in this century, regardless of whether they were for or against Hitler, National Socialism has been the main experience. When certain events took place in 1958 that did not conform with the new democratic outlook, the argument over National Socialism, which appeared to have been settled, suddenly became a problem again. A problem that included the fact that the youth had not itself experienced those days. Of course, they had grown up in the shadow of 1945, but what could they know about the matter?

Then the high officials also remembered the problem. The

schools were more strictly required to present a clearer treatment of recent history, and in the judicial field trials were begun that were long overdue if one really clung to the belief that such trials could pierce through to the heart of the past and unmask the guilty. It was especially embarrassing for West German judiciary that at times East German evidence had to be accepted which proved that judges and attorneys still practiced whose names had been connected with cold-blooded murder during the National Socialist period. This was merely a symptom of how little attention had been paid to these matters between 1949 and 1959. It goes without saying that the Ulbricht regime, especially, has no right at all to raise objections in this matter.

Basically, the problems that face the West Germans today are those that confront every state striving for a free form of government. The relation between citizen and state is complicated, and it is getting to be even more complicated the more the leadership of the state demands specialized knowledge, and the more technology and economics follow their own laws. The relationship of the citizen to the state in Germany since 1945 has become to a large degree the relationship of youth and its problems to the state. Though some of the youth after 1945 still believed in the realization of high ideals, even if it was a modified belief, skepticism had taken hold of most of them.

After 1918 a German historian expressed this. He referred to what he called the experience of the front-line soldier, which has taught that "an idea does not count for anything as compared with actual fact, but that the present moment, which is born of an idea, counts for everything." [7]

Here I shall again return to the historian Meinecke, who in 1925 had tried to make clear to the students in Berlin that it is void in politics to look upon the lesser evil as good and to defend it [8] As long as man engages in politics, determining the affairs of peoples and states, he will bring his mistakes and passions into politics with him. The apparent perfection of dictatorship is completely hollow and deceitful. A democracy —it does not have to possess the exact form of the present Federal Republic, but it must realize the citizen's state— whatever it may be, a democracy or a citizen's state is always at its beginning, it is never completely secure, and always needs the active participation of all its citizens.

The fifty years surveyed here have brought much passion and much suffering to Germany, at any rate tremendous changes such as few other nations have experienced. A world has been changed; the people have been changed. We saw that people who had hoped for survival and who lived to see 1945 often took as their first goal the cultivation of old values in the narrow confines of their families and friends. But this will not suffice—everyone individually is also responsible for his larger circle. The larger circle is still first of all the state, the Fatherland. No one can give Germany to the Germans, and no one can question their right to it, but neither can anyone rescue them from it. The younger generation has grown into it, into a heritage from which they cannot escape. To be sure, they are not the founders of this heritage, but they are responsible for it in the sense that they can shape it for the future. Only by working for the future can the past be "overcome." Actually the past makes sense only through what happens in the future. Nothing is unchangeable, no person and no country is lost as long as life still flickers in it. But the best way to give meaning to life today is by the endeavor to make the past experiences of the nation fruitful, and to extend that fruitfulness beyond the nation to mankind in the lasting struggle for freedom.[9]

Notes

In this English translation the notes that are useful only to German students have been omitted. The publisher of the English edition has included some notes to give brief and essential information on people and terms that would be unfamiliar to the present English speaking reader. These are marked EDITOR'S NOTE.

Introduction

1. Rudolf Häussler, *Die Stimme des Menschen* (H. W. Bähr, 1961), p. 21. Letters and sketches from all over the world, 1939–1945.
2. See p. 45 for definition of "stab in the back." [EDITOR'S NOTE]

Chapter One: The German People on the Eve of World War I

1. It is difficult to see in just retrospect the political and social conditions of the years before 1914, as an attempt to compare the memoirs of socialists and of conservatives or of those of the upper middle class will prove. Letters written during this period are more reliable. Among them are those of Elly Heuss-Knapp, *Bürgerin zweier Welten.* Compare these with my essay "Deutsche Briefe aus sechs Jahrzehnten," *Die Welt als Geschichte* (1962), Vol. XXII. All such letters, which should, of course, be read in conjunction with those of 1911, testify against the generalizations made about the last years of the monarchy. They refute the image of a state supposedly

governed by "absolute power" and also the primitive reverence paid to it.

2. See p. 29 for definition of three-class voting system. [EDITOR'S NOTE]

Chapter Two: The Germans and World War I

1. Theodor Heuss, 1884–1963, was first a writer and a newspaper editor, and then became professor of political science at the Technical University in Berlin. He was closely associated with Friedrich Naumann (Chapter IV, n. 15), with whom he edited *Hilfe,* and was a member of the Democratic party during the Weimar Republic. His liberal ideas made him unpopular with the National Socialists and he lived in retirement until after World War II. During this time he was supported by his wife. In 1945, he became cultural minister for Baden-Württemberg and professor at the Technical University of Stuttgart and also was a leader of the Free Democratic party. In 1949 he was elected the Federal Republic's first president.

His wife, Elly Heuss, was the daughter of the well-known political economist and financial theorist Friedrich Knapp. [EDITOR'S NOTE]

2. Elly Heuss-Knapp, *Bürgerin zweier Welten* (Marg. Vater, 1961), p. 146. A life as seen in letters and sketches.

3. *Der deutsche Soldat* (Rudolf Hoffmann, 1937), p. 10. Letters from the World War. A memorial.

4. *Ibid.,* p. 23.

5. *Ibid.,* p. 31.

6. *Ibid.,* p. 32.

7. *Ibid.,* pp. 61 and 102.

8. Heuss-Knapp, *Bürgerin zweier Welten,* p. 150 ff.

9. *Der deutsche Soldat,* p. 256.

10. Franz Marc, *Briefe aus dem Feld* (1940), p. 84.

In the United States the expression "fourth estate" has come to mean the press. Marc used the term as a derivation from its original meaning; he was referring to the working class. [EDITOR'S NOTE]

11. *Kriegsbriefe gefallener Studenten* (Ph. Witkop), p. 122. The year 1918 and later.

12. From the disturbing poem by Franz Werfel, "Der Krieg," in *Menschheitsdämmerung* (Kurt Pinthus, 1920). This excerpt is from a new edition (Rohwolt Taschenbuch, 1959), p. 82 ff.

13. In February 1915, the German government announced that in a "war zone" around the British Isles all enemy merchant shipping would be attacked and warned that neutral ships would proceed in the zone at their own risk. This declaration of limited submarine warfare brought an outcry of protest from neutrals, particularly from the United States. The sinking of the Cunard liner *Lusitania* did much to harden American feeling against Germany. The German government wavered a little and offered, under conditions, to moderate its policy, but on January 31, 1917, announced that it would enter on full-scale unrestricted submarine warfare not limited to a war zone. The United States in direct reply adopted a policy of "armed neutrality," which was a prelude to a declaration of war on April 6, 1917. [EDITOR'S NOTE]

14. *Der deutsche Soldat,* p. 445.

15. *Kriegsbriefe gefallener Studenten,* p. 352.

16. Erich von Ludendorff, 1865-1937, was one of the leading commanders in World War I, serving through the war as chief of staff to Field Marshal Hindenburg. His successes on the eastern front made him a hero throughout Germany. When he advised that Germany should ask for an armistice in 1918 he was dismissed. In 1920 he took part in the Kapp Putsch, and in 1923 in the Hitler Putsch. Later he became a National Socialist member of the Reichstag and, under the influence of his wife, joined other radical rightist movements. Toward the end of his life he became mentally unbalanced. [EDITOR'S NOTE]

17. Tannenberg, East Prussia, was the scene of a famous battle, on August 1914, in which Hindenburg and Ludendorff distinguished themselves by winning a decisive victory over the Russians. It is still regarded as one of the greatest encirclement operations in modern military history. [EDITOR'S NOTE]

18. Fritz Ernst, "Friedrich Ebert," *Ruperto Carola,* XIV (1962), 30-39.

19. On the whole it can be said that those who tend to reactionary viewpoints have to this day not grasped the full significance of the problems, especially of two: the consequences of the occupation of Belgium and those resulting from the refusal to grant Prussia equal franchise.

20. The question of Germany's acceptance of the parliamentary system is purposely anticipated here. It seems to me today, even

when looking back to 1918, the problem is treated too lightly. I discussed the problem in my speech at the jubilee celebrations of the Stuttgart Landtag in 1957. It was printed in *Drucksachen des Landtags von Baden-Württemberg, 1957,* and in *Zeitschrift für Württembergische Landesgeschichte,* Vol. XVII (1958). The devastating consequences of practically unrestrained criticism of the form of government during the Weimar Republic made a lasting impression, and, therefore, the franchise is nearly the only problem of parliamentarianism seriously discussed in Germany today.

21. Karl Jaspers, 1883–, was a professor of philosophy and psychology at the University of Heidelberg, where he also served as rector after World War II, until he left Germany in 1949 to become a professor at the University of Basel, Switzerland. Jaspers is generally considered one of the greatest of modern philosophers. His theories concerning the individual and existence have had great influence, particularly—with the teachings of Martin Heidegger—on the growth of Existentialism. Like many other leading intellectuals, he opposed the National Socialist regime. In 1945 he founded *Die Wandlung* together with Alfred Weker and Dolf Steinberg. In this periodical informative reports and political articles were published with the intention of giving Germans a political education that would enable them to guard their political rights. [EDITOR'S NOTE]

22. Karl Jaspers, *Max Weber* (1932, reprinted 1946); also Jaspers's memorial speech, first printed in 1921, now in Jaspers, *Rechenschaft und Ausblick* (1951). Speeches and essays. Marianne Weber, *Max Weber* (1926). A portrait. Theodor Heuss, "Max Weber in seiner Gegenwart," in Max Weber, *Gesammelte Politische Schriften* (2d ed., 1958).

23. Dueling among German university students became formalized in the period following the Napoleonic era. It had a definitely patriotic aspect at a time when Germany was recovering from defeat and humiliation. "Grudge duels" were at one time common among members of "fighting fraternities." Today dueling is carried on by comparatively few organizations and then on an intramural basis. [EDITOR'S NOTE]

24. From a lecture given by Weber in October 1916. Weber, *Gesammelte Politische Schriften* (2d ed.), p. 172.

25. In the Seven Years War, 1756–63, Maria Theresa of Austria and Frederick II of Prussia contested possession of the province of Silesia. In spite of several defeats, Frederick the Great also won brilliant victories and was successful in retaining Silesia for Prussia and thus elevated Prussia to a world military power. [EDITOR'S NOTE]

26. Weber, *Gesammelte Politische Schriften* (1st ed., 1921), p. 459. In 1st ed. only.

27. Marianne Weber, *Max Weber*, p. 544.

28. *Ibid.*, p. 568.

29. This mood, too, is reflected in the writings and letters of Max Weber. With regard to the franchise he writes, in May 1917, in a letter to Naumann: "The Pan-Germans can be defeated if peace comes soon and if the government makes the following statement concerning Prussia: 'The franchise rights of no man who went to war shall be inferior to those of anyone who remained at home.'" *Gesammelte Politische Schriften*, p. 472. In 1st ed. only.

30. Marianne Weber, *Max Weber*, p. 596.

31. In order to understand Weber's views correctly, one must follow the slow crystallization of his arguments in favor of parliamentarianism, especially those directed toward the opponents whom Weber hoped to isolate by this means.

32. Friedrich Meinecke, 1862–1954, was born in Prussia. He was professor at the University of Strassburg in 1901, and at Freiburg in 1906. During 1914–28 he was editor of the *Historische Zeitschrift* in Berlin. He was a liberal democrat who rejected National Socialism and figured prominently in the development of a historical perspective concerning Germany's history. In 1948 he became honorary rector at the Free University in Berlin. [EDITOR'S NOTE]

33. Friedrich Meinecke, *Politische Schriften und Reden* (G. Kotowski, 1958), pp. 225 and 255.

Chapter Three: Revolution, Armistice, and Versailles

1. The Germans called their flag simply "Schwartz-Weiss-Rot." Black, white, and red were the colors of the Bismarckian period. See p. 50 and n. 18 for other symbolic meanings of these colors. [EDITOR'S NOTE]

2. Never has so much remained unclarified as in the public debate

over the causes of the mutiny in the navy, and never has so much been obscured. In a certain sense, this helped create a "national" legend. But historically speaking, the significant fact remains that neither the officers nor the crews of the big ships had weathered the long period of inactivity without a decline in morale. No doubt agitation against military service existed in varying degrees on some ships. Certainly, the wide spread paralysis prevalent at that time in Germany's leading classes showed up most clearly in the navy.

3. From a poem by Karl Förster, "Erinnerung und Hoffnung."

4. Wilhelm Groener, 1867–1939, was a prominent general in World War I, and after the armistice he brought the troops home safely and well organized. He cooperated with Friedrich Ebert in preventing a Communist dictatorship from succeeding in Germany. He was a member of the Democratic party, served as minister of communications during 1920–23, and as minister of defense from 1928 to 32. He was dismissed by Hindenburg because of the strenuous measures he directed against the National Socialist storm-troopers. [EDITOR'S NOTE]

5. At a meeting of the state secretaries on November 5th, a report by Groener had made it clear that military resistance could "last only a little longer."

6. Philipp Scheidemann, 1865–1939, was a journalist and editor of socialist papers. He was an active Social Democrat and became leader of that party in the Reichstag. In 1918, he had been secretary of state without portfolio in the cabinet of Prince Max von Baden when he proclaimed the republic on November 9, 1918. He served as the republic's first chancellor until June 1919, and as a member of the Reichstag until 1933, when he left Germany. [EDITOR'S NOTE]

7. The different temperaments of the two moderate socialist leaders, Ebert and Scheidemann, repeatedly made themselves felt. We have only Scheidemann's memoirs (1928). For Ebert's attitude toward memoirs, see Fritz Ernst, "Friedrich Ebert," *Ruperto Carola*, XIV, 39.

8. The Freikorps was organized after World War I, when Noske was the minister of defense (see n. 11) and had the backing of the industrialists and landowners. The Freikorps consisted of volunteers, mostly young men who were violently nationalistic. They were assigned to police the borders, to keep order in the East and in the

Baltic area, and they were also used against rioters in Germany itself. In Berlin, on May 1 and 2, 1919, they fought with ruthless brutality and removed the danger that Communists would take over the government. The Freikorps was dissolved by the terms of the Treaty of Versailles which required the removal of all German troops from foreign territory. [EDITOR'S NOTE]

9. The Treaty of Brest-Litovsk was concluded between the Central Powers and Russia on March 3, 1918. Russia was forced to recognize the independence of Poland, the Baltic States, Georgia, and the Ukraine; Germany was to occupy Belorussia, and certain other territory was ceded to Turkey. In addition Russia was to pay an indemnity of 300,000,000 gold rubles. This treaty was annulled by the Treaty of Versailles. [EDITOR'S NOTE]

10. Friedrich Ebert, 1871–1925, was an active trade unionist in his youth. He became a member of the Social Democratic party in Bremen, and went to Berlin in 1905, where he became the secretary of the party's central committee. In 1912 he was elected to the Reichstag and in 1913 became party leader. In 1919 the national assembly at Weimar elected him president of the new German republic. During his presidency Germany accepted the Treaty of Versailles and adopted the Weimar Constitution. He won the respect of the middle class, but lost some of the support of his own party. He was not a revolutionary; Theodor Heuss called him "The Abraham Lincoln of German history." When he died in 1925 he was succeeded by Field Marshal von Hindenburg. [EDITOR'S NOTE]

11. Gustav Noske, 1868–1946, was a Social Democratic member of the Reichstag from 1906 to 1920. He was minister of defense in Friedrich Ebert's cabinet 1919–1920, but resigned after the Kapp Putsch. He organized the Freikorps and ruthlessly suppressed leftist and Communist uprisings. From 1920 on he was governor of Hanover, but was ousted in 1933 by the National Socialists. In 1944 he was arrested on the suspicion that he had participated in the plot against Hitler and was released by the Russian troops in 1945. [EDITOR'S NOTE]

12. Since 1945 the question—Germany's blame for World War I —which was so one-sidedly illuminated by Hitler's attitude, has, in general, been treated with more hesitancy. For us it is important to note that after the end of the war, the fight against the "war-guilt

lie" united groups of Germans for a common national objective who otherwise would have had little in common with each other. The political groups on the Left were, however, essentially more restrained in their public struggle against the war-guilt thesis of the enemy than those on the Right. The government itself refrained for the time being from issuing a public declaration along this line, because the treaty had been signed, and the amounts of the reparations payments had still to be settled, giving the former enemy the means to exercise pressure. Perhaps the leftist groups would have made a public declaration had they sensed the important relationship between this question and the continuing political unrest in the country.

13. For a discussion of the "stab in the back" see Fritz Ernst, "Zum Ende des Ersten Weltkrieges," *Die Welt als Geschichte* (1957), Vol. XVII.

14. It was not the result of one-sided and intentionally false war propaganda that made the German people believe in the possibility of victory up to the fall of 1918; the military leaders of Germany shared this belief up to the month of August. It is difficult for unbiased young people today to conceive of this, because they have grown up in the awareness of the might of the United States of America. But Hindenburg and Ludendorff did not realize, up to the summer of 1918, how significant the fact was that American troop transports were bringing great numbers of fresh troops practically unhindered into France. We must understand clearly that part of the older generation—admittedly a small part—knows little of the real situation even today, and, therefore, must seek refuge in the "stab in the back" theory.

15. Rumania had proclaimed its neutrality at the outbreak of World War I, but had joined the Allied camp in 1916. Austro-German forces soon overran the country, and in February 1918 Rumania had to consent to a harsh peace treaty. But in November 1918 Allied troops came to the rescue, and Rumania resumed its fight against the Central Powers just as the war was ending. [EDITOR'S NOTE]

16. The burden of compulsory military service imposed by an unloved regime was only understood by the German middle class during the National Socialist period.

17. Germany's army was abolished and German armed forces

limited to 100,000 men by the provisions of the Treaty of Versailles. In order to train a larger body of men who could be mobilized in the event of an emergency, secret military training was given to a number of younger men in what was called the "black army." [EDITOR'S NOTE]

18. In the end the colors of the Weimar Republic flag were the Black-Red-and-Gold for the national flag and, as a compromise, Black-White-and-Red with the national colors in the upper corner, for the merchant flag. The colors Black-White-and-Red were associated with the Bismarckian Reich, and the colors Red-Black-and-Gold, representative of the revolution of 1848, date back to the Turngemeinden (sports associations) and Burschenschaften (fraternities) first organized by Friedrich Ludwig Jahn in 1815 with the aim of making German students strive for idealistic and nationalistic unity. [EDITOR'S NOTE]

19. For Kapp Putsch see n. 1 of Chapter IV. [EDITOR'S NOTE]

Chapter Four: The Weimar Republic

1. Wolfgang Kapp, 1858–1922, was active in the Prussian government and founded the "Fatherland party" in 1917. He led the radical rightist elements who tried to overthrow the government in 1920 in the abortive Kapp Putsch, and died while awaiting trial. [EDITOR'S NOTE]

2. The Putsch was hastily broken up. Its leaders did not agree about its goals. But one cannot understand the reason for the Putsch without realizing clearly how much "combustible" nationalist material was lying around. But the nationalist groups had lost their sense of reality ever since 1918. It frequently happened that the bold assertions that men made to their regular buddies in taverns were mistaken for the exultation of the people. The disbandment of military units was not the only incentive to action; especially critical minds were uneasy about the by no means laudable part played by the upper classes of Germany in 1918, who in 1914 had been so sure of themselves. The slogan of 1918, that weapons should not be used against the mutineers, must have seemed humiliating when soberly compared with the situation and with the mood of 1914. Here was one of the prerequisites for the rise of Hitler. He not

only attacked the "November criminals" but also the failure of the upper classes, and he thereby expressed what many felt, especially the less sophisticated segments of the people. This was the condition that necessarily led to his combining nationalism and socialism, at least as far as the framework of the tactical situation of the period after 1920 is concerned.

3. The fact that Noske, who in leftist circles as well as in his own party was regarded with distrust because of his confidence in the officers, now declared that he had been mistaken in his trust contributed much to the breach between the government and the army. A breach that grew larger during the Gessler-Seeckt era, for which, by the way, Gessler was certainly not to blame.

4. Heuss-Knapp, *Bürgerin zweier Welten*, p. 179.

5. A. S. Makarenkow, "Ein Pädagogisches Poem" (1935; published in German as *Der Weg ins Leben*). Also other didactic stories, and his *Book for Parents* (1937; in German 1952).

6. "Der Stahlhelm. Bund der Frontsoldaten" (Steel Helmet: Union of the Soldiers who had been at the Front) was founded in November 1918. The steel helmet had already been used as a symbol at home, in war pictures and on posters used in the campaign for war loans. It was later used in the sense mentioned in the text even outside the Bund der Frontsoldaten.

7. The Guelphs were a German princely family who became prominent early in the Middle Ages. In the times of Emperor Otto IV (a Guelph) and Frederick IV and later, the family name was given to a party (the Guelphs) which supported the papacy against the imperial party (the Ghibellines). In later German history branches of the family remained important. One branch ruled Hanover until 1866, when the Hanoverian king, George V, was deposed, and the state was annexed to Prussia. The group that continued to oppose Prussian rule kept alive the name Guelph. They joined the Catholic Centrists under Ludwig Windthorst to oppose Bismarck. In the Weimar Republic the Guelphs formed a tiny splinter party in the Reichstag, and often joined with other traditionalist opposition groups. [EDITOR'S NOTE]

8. That a social form of antisemitism still existed in the Officers' Corps in 1918 and that Jews were not supposed to become officers is shown by a statement made by the man chosen to be the chief of

demobilization, Walter Reinhardt, issued on November 3, 1918. In it, he made it clear that as far as the Jewish question was concerned he was for granting them "full rights, even commissions as officers," although the Prussian minister of war most probably expected a different attitude of him in his new capacity.

9. The HAPAG (Hamburg-American Paket Aktien Gesellschaft) was one of the German steamship lines that was well known before World War II. Together with North-German Lloyd it operated passenger ships between Germany and North America, but lost most of its ships in World War II. [EDITOR'S NOTE]

10. In the socialist camp the anxiety over the eight-hour day was well justified. Heavy industry was trying to abolish it in the fall of 1923. Industrialists asked the French army to help enforce a compulsory prolongation of the working day, but the request was refused.

11. Pankow is a district in the northern part of Berlin and is the seat of the president of the German Democratic Republic. The "Eastern zone," is governed by officials who are members of the Socialist Unity Party, the only party permitted to exist, and is a key state of the group of Communist satellite countries in Eastern Europe. [EDITOR'S NOTE]

12. The Independent Social Democrats split off from the regular Social Democrats in December 1915 because they opposed the continuation of the war and refused to vote for the war credits. At the end of the war a radical wing of the Independent Social Democrats, calling itself the Spartacus League, led by Rosa Luxemburg and Karl Liebknecht, founded the German Communist party. [EDITOR'S NOTE]

13. His own book, *Mein Kampf,* reveals how Hitler, as politician, wished to be thought of. However, neither *Mein Kampf* nor his published speeches nor the statements he made in conversations make an immediate impression upon the generation that did not know him from personal experience. Of course the danger exists that a "demythologized" Hitler may become incomprehensible if one does not capture the effect he had upon many of his contemporaries. The sources for this are not easily accessible today. I am thinking of the reports in independent foreign newspapers on the Hitler-meetings, and of the testimony given by his former followers at the trials that have taken place since 1945—in this case, of course, with

the limitation that many of the accused were trying to exonerate themselves.

14. Nationalsozialistische Deutsche Arbeiterpartei (NSDAP). Probably no other name could have been devised for the movement led by Hitler that combined so ingeniously the three aspects included in this title: nationalism, socialism, and labor. It was on February 24, 1920 that Hitler announced the Twenty-five Points of the National Socialist German Labor party, and from that date the German Labor party was called by that name. [EDITOR'S NOTE]

15. Friedrich Naumann, 1860–1919, was a politician with liberal, idealistic, and socialist views. He was the first president of the National Socialist Union, which he helped found in 1896. (It had nothing to do with Hitler's party.) He was a member of the Reichstag 1907–1912, 1913–1918, and founder and editor of the *Hilfe*. [EDITOR'S NOTE]

16. The Treaty of Rapallo was an agreement made between Germany and Russia in 1922. It restored diplomatic and commercial relations between the two nations. One of its by-products was that Russia now secretly produced arms for Germany, which Germany had been forbidden to produce under the Treaty of Versailles. [EDITOR'S NOTE]

17. Germany, France, Belgium, England, Italy, Czechoslovakia, and Poland entered into an agreement in 1925 in Locarno, Switzerland, which aimed at guaranteeing peace in Europe. Among other things, the pact endorsed and strengthened the Treaty of Versailles, stipulated that Germany should submit the settlement of its eastern boundaries to arbitration, and guaranteed Germany's entry into the League of Nations. [EDITOR'S NOTE]

18. Stresemann earned the hostility of the Right by his foreign policy. They accused him of betraying his old ideals. He had emphasized Germany's peaceful intentions, but how little he had surrendered of his old ideals was not apparent until his estate was released. Until then only a short extract, which was calculated to be appropriate under the circumstances, was printed in the three-volume work *Vermächtnis* (1932–33). It would be primitive, however, to regard him as a mere opportunist. At any rate he did what at the time could be done for the national power of Germany. Those

who discredited him while he was still alive later became grist for Hitler's mill. Twenty years after Locarno Hitler committed suicide.

19. In 1824 Prussia had gained control over the Lower Rhineland by giving up certain of its Polish provinces. Although it was separated from Prussia proper by Saxony, the acquisition of this territory enabled Prussia to gain supremacy in industry and commerce. [EDITOR'S NOTE]

20. There is no critical biography of Hindenburg containing references. It must not be forgotten that even in 1932 the leaders of the Social Democrats, even though they were in an embarrassing position, felt compelled to support his candidacy for reelection. They apparently did not have too bad an impression of the way he had conducted his office up to that time. The fact that in January of the following year, after the downfall of Schleicher and certainly under the most unfortunate influences, he opened the way for the leader of the strongest party (a course which he could scarcely have avoided under parliamentary regulations) cannot be evaluated by itself. One must compare his acts with the acts of the republicans of that time—the conduct of Braun and of Severing in Prussia, and also the blindness of Hugenberg and of Papen.

21. The years after 1925 are actually the most deceptive in the history of the Weimar Republic. Viewed externally, the radicalization of the rightist groups seemed to have come to an end. This was also reported by the inspector in charge of the supervision of law and order.

22. Weber, *Gesammelte Politische Schriften,* p. 381. (2d ed., p. 476.) (From the *Frankfurter Zeitung* of January 17, 1919.)

23. Marianne Weber, *Max Weber,* p. 640.

24. *Ibid.,* p. 642 ff.

25. Weber, *Gesammelte Politische Schriften,* p. 482. In 1st ed. only.

26. Marianne Weber, *Max Weber,* p. 685.

27. Friedrich Meinecke, *Politische Schriften und Reden,* p. 365.

28. *Ibid.,* p. 370.

29. *Ibid.,* pp. 374 and 380 ff.

30. Charles G. Dawes, 1865–1951, was a statesman and financier who was elected vice president of the United States under Coolidge in 1924. In 1923–24 he was head of the reparations committee, and

presented the Dawes Plan that successfully adjusted the reparations payments of Germany in accordance with Germany's ability to pay. For this work he received the Nobel Prize. [EDITOR'S NOTE]

31. For the evaluation of Stresemann today it should be added that the new insights gained when his entire legacy had been made available led to remarkable criticisms—Stresemann was said to be an opportunist, and basically unreliable in international affairs. In fact, propaganda against the new Germany today is occasionally created by this means. But apart from the question whether the minister was congenial or not: what degree of personal devotion was actually expected of a statesman of the Weimar Republic, in order that it could be said he had lived up to those standards? Is it not clear that precisely such impossible demands can again kindle a new kind of German nationalism? The concessions allowed the defeated French after 1871 and 1940 should not be refused the Germans.

32. Actually this tendency was already noticeable in the elections of the first Reichstag of the republic in June 1920 (after the dissolution of the National Assembly). At that time the parties responsible for the government lost a third or more of their seats to the opposition on the Right *and* on the Left. It was to this that Elly Heuss referred in her remark that the nation was lurching to the Right and to the Left at the same time, and that any party which assumed responsibility for the government would expose itself to mud-slinging. In 1920 the basic problem of the republic was already evident in the votes cast in the election.

33. Alfred Hugenberg, 1865–1951, was a highly successful businessman. He became a member of the Reichstag in 1920 and was chairman of the extreme rightist German Nationalist party, from 1928 to 1933. He failed in his attempt to form a coalition of rightist parties to block Hitler's progress. He entered Hitler's allegedly coalition cabinet as minister of economics, but retired six months later, and was without political influence for the rest of his life. [EDITOR'S NOTE]

34. Harry Graf Kessler, *Tagebücher, 1918–1937* (1961), p. 660 ff. Fritz von Unruh was supposed to have said, "The chief reason for the downfall of the republic was . . . that they completely failed to appreciate the importance of the youthful and of the heroic in politics. Immediately after the war, in the early days of the republic,

he [Unruh] had recognized (and that is true) the strategic importance of these two factors for the new state. He had preached it to all influential parties, especially to his friend, the Prussian minister of culture, Becker. But his ideas were completely misunderstood and rejected by all. They were not taken seriously and were considered to be of no consequence." (April 25, 1932).

35. Harry Graf Kessler, 1868–1937, was writer and publisher. He founded the Cranach Press in Weimar and served for a time in the diplomatic corps. His works include a book about the League of Nations, a biography of Walther Rathenau, and his memoirs.

Fritz von Unruh, 1895–, is a dramatic poet, and a prominent literary figure of republican Germany. He was an officer in World War I and emerged from the war a confirmed pacifist. His early expressionist work includes antiwar propaganda and a warning against dictatorship. He left Germany in 1933, and returned in 1947. [EDITOR'S NOTE]

36. The SA, STURMABTEILUNG [storm troops] was the original private army organized by Hitler from which the various branches of the SS later developed. The SA wore brown shirts and at first fought in the political street brawls staged by the National Socialists, and policed party meetings. But in 1934 the SA lost its political significance— Hitler had its leader, Ernst Röhm, and other prominent members killed in the "Blood Purge"—and it became simply an organization to give German youth its premilitary training. The SS, SCHUTZSTAFFEL [security echelon] developed after 1929 under Heinrich Himmler into National Socialism's most dangerous henchmen. They were considered the "elite" troops and stood under rigid discipline. They wore black uniforms. At first the SS consisted of volunteers, but later their numbers were increased by conscription. The SS were in charge of the concentration camps, served as Hitler's personal guard, and functioned as secret police. One section, the Waffen SS [weapons SS] fought with the regular army. The GESTAPO, GEHEIM STAATS-POLIZEI [secret state police] was founded in 1933 by the National Socialists and was headed by Hermann Göring. In 1936 the SS and the Gestapo were united under Heinrich Himmler, and the Gestapo was supplanted by the SD, Sicherheitsdienst [security service] of the SS. More, however, was known about the atrocious activities of the Gestapo than about those of the SD. HJ, HITLER JUGEND [Hitler

Youth], and BDM, BUND DEUTSCHER MÄDCHEN [Union of German Girls] were the youth movements with which Hitler displaced all other youth movements in Germany during the National Socialist period. [EDITOR'S NOTE]

Chapter Five: World War I in Literary Retrospect

1. Without the literary surge that began some ten years after the war, it is impossible to understand the world between the wars. This literature again brought the impressions and experiences of the war to the forefront. Books such as those written by Remarque and Renn introduced the youth, who had not lived through it, to the war. But, on the other hand, the political effect of this literary surge should not be overestimated. The fundamental tone of the leading books was pacifistic or, at least, did not support war. But it had become clear that the need for the heroic of which Meinecke and Unruh spoke, prevailed in the life of the youth, at least among those who were of the middle class in its wider sense, though, of course, it was a somewhat playful heroism that merely filled a vacuum in the make-up of the youth.

2. Erich Maria Remarque, 1897–, was born in Osnabruck, Westphalia, a descendant of French immigrants who settled in the Rhineland during the French Revolution. The belief that Remarque is a pseudonym is widespread, but not true. It was one of the rumors spread about him during the National Socialist regime in order to discredit Remarque's standing with the German people. [EDITOR'S NOTE]

3. Because of its contents, Zweig's book belongs only to the very fringe of books dealing with the effect of the war in the West. But the success of this book shows that in 1927 one could use the war as subject matter without arousing prevalent political passions.

4. The chief difference between one-year volunteers and regular volunteers in Germany was that the one-year volunteers paid their own expenses (uniforms, lodgings, food, etc.), whereas the regular volunteers did not. [EDITOR'S NOTE]

5. This does not mean, however, that Grimm must be placed in the same category with such authors as Hitler and Goebbels. Grimm has a completely idealistic conception of the German. But the end

of his hero, who becomes a martyr of a not very clearly defined National Socialism, does not do justice to the quality of the work as a whole. Here the epic becomes a political tract.

6. It is especially instructive to note in Hitler's descriptions of the war how he compares his encounter with the British in the field with the image that German propaganda has given of them, "At that time I became aware of the usefulness of this form of propaganda for the first time." Many of the middle-class readers of the book who were quite prepared to become Hitler enthusiasts did not sense that one of the strongest emotions in this emotion-charged work was hostility toward the middle class. Hitler considered the middle class responsible for the entire German conduct during World War I (including the stupid anti-English propaganda), and for their failure to solve the big problems. "The destiny of nations cannot be changed with kid gloves." And referring to 1923, "At that time I became keenly conscious of the fact that the German middle class had accomplished its mission and that it was not destined to perform any more tasks." (Both quotations occur in *Notwehr als Recht,* Vol. II, Chap. 15.) In England Neville Chamberlain had been censured for not understanding Hitler, but he had an excuse a complete English translation of *Mein Kampf* did not appear until the winter of 1938–39; Hugenberg, Papen, and others did not have the excuse of a language problem. An exposition should be written in this connection that discusses the fact that the rightist middle class misunderstood Hitler up to the very point of no return, and should not only expose the reactionaries but also the leading members of a group that was very important before 1933, the Tatkreis, the action group.

Chapter Six: The End of the Republic

1. The "emergency decrees" were incorporated in Article 48 of the Weimar Constitution and empowered the president of the republic to restore order by decree if sudden disturbances occurred to threaten public safety. They also enabled him to suspend temporarily the fundamental rights guaranteed by the Constitution. These presidential orders and decrees had to be countersigned by the chancellor and were to be rescinded at the demand of the Reichs-

tag. Brüning, under Hindenburg, extended the meaning of Article 48 by using the power it gave the president and the chancellor to pass measures that had been defeated in the Reichstag. In 1930 he dissolved the Reichstag, and working only with a presidential cabinet he continued to govern by decree. [EDITOR'S NOTE]

2. The Five Percent Clause, requiring that any party must gain at least five percent of the total vote at an election in order to be represented in the Reichstag, has contributed much to the elimination of small splinter parties that flourished in the Reichstag during the Weimar Republic. [EDITOR'S NOTE]

3. Horst Wessel was a member of the SA. He was killed in a brawl when National Socialism was in the early stages of its political career, and thus became a martyr for the National Socialist movement. [EDITOR'S NOTE]

4. After the Reichstag fire in February 1933, Hitler pushed through a Decree for the Protection of People and State, which, under the pretext of guarding against further actions of this kind, deprived the people of personal and civil rights and exposed them to the ruthlessness of the National Socialist regime. This decree was followed up, after the elections, by the Enabling Act whereby the Reichstag gave its power to the Reich cabinet, and so voted itself out of existence and gave Hitler the dictatorial power he wanted. [EDITOR'S NOTE]

5. That day at Potsdam brought the end of the parties. There had been evidence of decadence and fatigue in the parties; since 1929 they had no longer been in command of the changing situation, and they had no means with which to counteract the tactics of parades and uproar the NSDAP used in order to heighten the sense that a crisis existed. Around 1929–30 the argument over 1918 was still an important one. The unusual weariness of Hermann Müller can certainly be traced to the agitation that repeatedly flared up against him because he had signed the Versailles Treaty.

Chapter Seven: The Rule of Hitler

1. Karl Dönitz, 1891–1963, was commander of the submarine fleet from 1936 on and was made supreme commander of the German navy in 1943. Before committing suicide, Hitler designated Dönitz

head of state, and it was he and Jodl who signed the unconditional surrender. Dönitz was sentenced to ten years imprisonment at the Nürnberg trials. [EDITOR'S NOTE]

2. The German Christian church was set up under Ludwig Müller by the National Socialist leaders in an attempt to gain control over the Protestant sects. The attempt failed because of the ardent opposition of a group of Protestants, lead by Martin Niemoeller, commonly called the Confessional church. [EDITOR'S NOTE]

3. See n. 2.

4. Both leading Christian denominations find it difficult to expound their stand under the dictatorship. Naturally each has its own characteristic difficulties. For the Evangelical church it is important, first of all, to correct and to supplement the Niemoeller group's somewhat one-sided view. In the Catholic Church the question raised is why the hierarchy within Germany and abroad did not oppose the dictatorship from the start. The prevalence of optimism at the beginning amazes both of the churches as well as other groups today, though the circumstances that led to it are well understood. Bishop Wurm and the Niemoeller brothers on the Protestant side, and some bishops and, to a certain extent, the Vatican on the Catholic side, may be counted among those optimists. By no means should one criticize specific people on either side, no matter how prominent they were. In connection with the Vatican one must remember Fascism and the Lateran Treaty of 1929.

5. Great Britain, because Germany was building larger battleships than allowed in the Treaty of Versailles, secretly negotiated the Anglo-German Naval Agreement with Germany in 1935; this ensured that Germany's navy would not exceed one third the size of the British navy. It also gave the Germans the right to build submarines—up to 60 percent of the submarine strength of the British, or, if deemed necessary by Germans, an equal number. The Anglo-German Naval Agreement was a violation of the Versailles Treaty. [EDITOR'S NOTE]

6. In retrospect one must recall that in spite of the wrong that was perpetrated, the general impression in 1933 was that something was being done to meet the emergencies and, especially, unemployment. Even people who opposed dictatorship with all their might were caught up in this belief. The great energy that no doubt had

been at work also in the Brüning government was lost in the turmoil of counterpropaganda.

7. See Chapter IV, n. 36.

8. Martin Bormann was born in 1900. He was the artisan of many brutal practices used by National Socialists in dealing with the enemies of the Third Reich. It was in 1941 that he became prominent in party leadership, and at the time of Hitler's death he was second in command. He probably died in Berlin in 1945, but the circumstances of his death have never been fully established, and this has given rise to rumors that he is still living in Argentina or in some other South American country. Rudolf Hess, 1894–, was one of Hitler's early followers. He had been in prison with Hitler after the Putsch of 1923, and there Hitler dictated *Mein Kampf* to him. In 1939 Hitler named him his successor, second only to Göring. Hess is the man who stole an airplane in 1941 and flew to Scotland with the apparent intention of negotiating a peace treaty. He was arrested then, and at the Nürnberg trials was sentenced to life imprisonment. His sanity is still a disputed question. [EDITOR'S NOTE]

Chapter Eight: World War II

1. Again I refer you to the letters of Elly Heuss-Knapp in *Bürgerin zweier Welten*. This surge of internal resistance did not, by the way, last very long. However, it was clearly noticeable even among the National Socialists in Heidelberg. Apart from the primitive brutes only actual cowards held back in those days.

2. When in the summer of 1939 the leading National Socialist official at the University gave the farewell speech for the students who were going to help with the harvest, one of the National Socialists asked me whether I had noticed that no remark against Bolshevism had been made, as was usually the case. He then hinted that a settlement was being negotiated between Hitler and Stalin. When I remarked that this might evoke some difficulties among the followers of the Führer, he answered in what to him seemed to be a reassuring manner. Some weeks later it became apparent that he had been right, even in the assumption that the adherents would follow their Führer wherever he led them. The complete surprise that Hitler's reversal of the main policy of the National Socialists occasioned is

not dealt with sufficiently in many discussions. Of course, it was immediately covered up by the war against Poland that broke out one week after the pact with Moscow had been announced.

3. The Warthe region is west of the Polish Corridor. It derived its name from the Warthe river, which is a tributary of the Oder and was developed as an agricultural region by Frederick the Great. [EDITOR'S NOTE]

4. Even before his rise to power, Hitler's attitude toward England was as paradoxical as that of the majority of the German people. In fact one can compare it with the vindictive love the last Kaiser had for the British. The passages in *Mein Kampf* are well known. Whenever Hitler turned directly to England a similar tone becomes noticeable. But even in quite casual remarks his basic respect for the English can be seen. For example, in *Hitlers Lagebesprechungen: Die Protokollfragmente seiner militärischen Konferenzen 1942–1945* (Helmut Heiber, 1962), p. 61, Jodl reports that in Africa thirty-one parachutists had been captured, but that it was not certain whether they were American or English. Hitler replies: "The English don't let themselves be taken so easily, they are tough dogs." In the study of the pathology of the German conception of England, Hitler must not be omitted, both as the symptom and as the cause. At any rate, whenever Hitler openly expressed it, the hatred he felt for England was a bridge to numerous groups of the old German bourgeoisie. They sensed a continuation of their hatred, which they owed essentially to Tirpitz. The attitude toward France was much simpler, Hitler's as well as that of the German bourgeoisie.

5. After 1933 the Germans also knew too little about the basic concepts to recognize the similarity between the two systems. However, it was easy to discern that Fascism was much milder than National Socialism. Only around 1938, and then during the war itself, did the similarity between the terrorism that existed in Russia and in Germany become evident. Toward the end of the war it sometimes happened that Germans, taking refuge in illusions, believed the Russian system to be less severe than Hitler's—this illusion did not last long.

6. When evaluating the tangible plans (those that have survived) of the resistance fighters, the decisive point to look for is whether they show an awareness of the fact that since 1920 so much had

happened to the German people that any plans based on old conservative methods would no longer be effective. Though the plans of the conspirators have sometimes been analyzed, the attempt to analyze them in the light of the experiences that the younger generation had after 1933 has never been made.

7. Graf Claus Schenk von Stauffenberg, 1907–44, was chief of staff of the army reserve forces in 1944, and often participated in conferences with Hitler. He was among the most active leaders of the resistance, and it was he who planted the time bomb at Rastenburg. The bomb went off, but the explosion was not strong enough to kill Hitler because the conference on that day was not held in the usual solid concrete bunker, but in a room made partly of wood, and so the explosion was ineffective. [EDITOR'S NOTE]

8. It seems to me that a history of German emigration under Hitler is urgently needed. The point of departure can only be Germany itself. During extended visits abroad I have become widely acquainted with the fate of German emigrants in several countries, especially in the United States and in Great Britain. What gifts Hitler gave these countries, and how differently this is expressed in the individual destinies! Only the stubborn on both sides cannot see the historical relevance of this subject: The emigrants who want to forget their homeland as quickly as possible, and the narrow-minded provincials in Germany who have no interest in those spheres that were heavily depleted because of this emigration from Germany.

9. See Chapter IV, n. 36.

10. See Chapter IV, n. 36.

11. Germans advised the Americans while the law governing the German tribunals was being formulated. Either because they had poor memories, or because they were too weak, these Germans did not succeed in explaining clearly all the intricacies of the system prevalent from 1933 to 1945 to the American authorities. Joining the NSDAP had, of course, been a serious step, but those of us who had not taken it knew very well that wide discrepancies existed among the members. We also knew that some nonmembers could be more dangerous to the critic than many a party member, particularly those whose application for membership had been rejected.

12. Anyone who, like myself, had just become a lecturer at a German university in 1933 will never forget what a shock it was to see

some of the professors of the older generation who enjoyed a great scholastic reputation bend rather easily to the demands and to the language of the National Socialists. Whatever it was that played a decisive part in this—hatred of the Weimar Republic, cowardliness, or the usual illusions of middle-class rightists concerning the character of National Socialism—these older colleagues had no idea what the university and what scholarship meant to us younger ones.

13. When an attempt is made to reach a historical judgment in connection with National Socialism, I feel that the danger I discussed in the Preface and in the Introduction must be seriously taken into account. Anyone who does not try to imagine the atmosphere of that period will see everything as shallow and pale—merely a period of crime—the human element having escaped from the picture. In such a light, however, the period cannot be understood and becomes incredible. Those who lived through it, whatever their personal circumstances were, turn away embittered from such descriptions. Movies in which members of the National Socialist party appear only as criminals also have a devastating effect. The actual crimes were terrible enough, but not so much was known about them as the victors, and especially the Americans, assumed in 1945. How much inward and outward participation in these crimes there was is difficult to establish in individual cases, as is shown by some of the flagrant cases with which the courts are still involved today.

Chapter Nine: From 1945 until 1961

1. At the same time it must be stated that in the beginning the Russian occupation was supported by many non-Communists partly because of a general anti-Fascist attitude and partly because they were aware of the misery that the German occupation had brought to Russia (which had hardly been mitigated by the proper conduct of many German military units).

2. For the psychological bases of the American occupation policy —as much as could be gleaned from American thought itself on the German picture—see Fritz Ernst, "Blick auf Deutschland," *Die Welt als Geschichte* (1950), Vol. X and (1955), Vol. XV.

3. Henry Morgenthau Jr., 1891–, was Secretary of the Treasury of the United States from 1935 to 1945. In 1945 he outlined a plan

whereby industrialized Germany was to be converted into an agricultural nation without upsetting its economy. According to this plan the Allies would be able to control Germany and prevent it from again becoming powerful in arms. Consideration of the plan was soon abandoned. [EDITOR'S NOTE]

4. Häussler, *Die Stimme des Menschen,* p. 322 ff. It continues: "I know many decent people, in officers' uniforms and among the soldiers, who are also burdened by the same skepticism as I. It seems to me that at no time did contempt for human beings reach such extremes."

5. The law that transferred the power and responsibility of the military government to the German tribunals in 1946 was part of the American denazification proceedings. The law stipulated that all Germans over eighteen fill out a questionnaire. These questionnaires were then sorted into one of five categories, ranging from major offenders to those who were exonerated. [EDITOR'S NOTE]

6. The Americans and most of the Germans who were active in the denazification process had remarkably wrong ideas. They believed that what had to be done at once was to stamp out the National Socialist "poison," and they talked about how much of it "still" existed. Actually, the expurgation of the Hitler-faith had begun long before the arrival of the occupation forces; it had made the greatest progress when Hitler's suicide and the desertion of his leading followers were announced. And to this must be added the impression made by the powerful armies of the enemy.

7. S. A. Kaehler, *Wilhelm von Humboldt und der Staat* (1927), p. 574, Epilogue.

8. Meinecke, *Politische Schriften,* p. 374.

9. Every reader will understand that I have been particularly careful in the last chapter. Much could yet be said, for instance, about the part the emigrants played as experts advising the military government, and the psychological significance this had; I could have discussed more fully the general mood of the Germans between 1945 and 1948. But it seemed to me that especially here it would be best to say little, since otherwise I would expose myself to the great danger of passing unjustified general judgments based upon personal experience. Thus I have essentially brought forward only what seemed most important. I am conscious of the fact that I have simplified matters here and throughout the book, but I felt it would be better to oversimplify than to say nothing at all.